RECORD STORE DAY ™

THE MOST IMPROBABLE COMEBACK OF THE 21ST CENTURY

By Larry Jaffee

RARE BIRD

Los Angeles, Calif.

RARE BIRD

THIS IS A GENUINE RARE BIRD BOOK

Rare Bird Books
6044 North Figueroa Street
Los Angeles, CA 90042
rarebirdbooks.com

FIRST TRADE PAPERBACK EDITION

Author photograph by Sedona Young

For more information, address:
Rare Bird Books Subsidiary Rights Department
6044 North Figueroa Street
Los Angeles, CA 90042

Set in Minion
Printed in the United States

10 9 8 7 6 5 4 3 2 1

Library of Congress Cataloging-in-Publication Data
Names: Jaffee, Larry, author.
Title: Record Store Day: the most improbable
comeback of the twenty-first century / by Larry Jaffee.
Description: First paperback edition. | Los Angeles : Rare Bird Books, 2022.
Identifiers: LCCN 2021047667 | ISBN 9781644282557 (paperback)
Subjects: LCSH: Record Store Day—History. | Record stores—History
—21st century. | Popular music—Marketing—History—21st century. |
Music—Marketing—History—21st century. | Sound recording
industry—History—21st century. | Sound recordings—History—21st century.
Classification: LCC ML36 .R434 2022 | DDC 306.4/8424—dc23

LC record available at https://lccn.loc.gov/2021047667

"What kind of heaven, is that you can't have your records?"
—Michael Chabon, *Telegraph Avenue*

This book is dedicated to my daughter Annie Jaffee, who apparently caught the vinyl gene from my DNA and one day is going to inherit a great record collection, as long as her big brother, Jake Jaffee, gets first dibs on the Black Sabbath LPs (even if he only hangs the covers on the wall).

CONTENTS

9 Foreword › by Kosmo Vinyl

15 Chapter One › *The Report of My Death Was an Exaggeration*

30 Chapter Two › *Noise in the Basement*

47 Chapter Three › *Do You Wanna Dance?*

58 Chapter Four › *Enter Metallica*

61 Chapter Five › *Message to Love*

74 Chapter Six › *Money Changes Everything*

82 Chapter Seven › *Wild World*

102 Chapter Eight › *The Under Assistant West Coast Promotion Man*

124 Chapter Nine › *Gimme More*

131 Chapter Ten › *Born to Run*

170 Chapter Eleven › *You Can't Always Get What You Want*

184 Chapter Twelve › *Rebel Rebel*

190 Chapter Thirteen › *Shake It Off*

204 Epilogue

208 Acknowledgments

211 Cast of Characters

FOREWORD

by Kosmo Vinyl

"A World Without Record Stores!" No, it's not a long-lost episode of *The Twilight Zone* nor an internet-published short story with millions of views. It was in 2007, and it was a very real possibility of what the future of recorded music might look like! That is until a small group of people got together and, under the banner "Record Store Day," decided to do something about it. Over fifteen years later, I am pleased to report that such a disaster has been averted. But the war is not won, and the battle continues.

Today, more than at any other time in history, more people have more access to more recorded music than ever before. The ever-expanding High Speed Access Wi-Fi World has given us more music than it is humanly possible to listen to. Titles by the thousands for more genres than most of us can even imagine—but how to make sense of it all? This is where the record store comes into its own; the very territory it has always occupied—a physical space that can help you figure out what to listen to. Familiar or unknown, large or small, organized or chaotic, it's the place where you can see, touch, feel, hear, and really get a sense of what a record is all about.

Sure you can get music by a click of the device of your choosing, but who declared convenience king? In the same way that hamburgers sold by a restaurant chain represented by a psychotic looking clown might be the most popular sources of cooked food, we all know it is far from the best you can get, especially locally. If you want the good stuff, you've got to go to the right place.

The record store is a whole world, filled with music, and you just enter through a door. A place that can take you anywhere you want to go or to some spot you'd never thought of going, filled with ideas, observations, and opinions. No passport, no visa, no ticket required. Even if you don't have any money, you can still go in and check it all out! The record store is where, more than anywhere else, I learned about the world beyond the one I actually lived in. It's also where I found my thoughts, fears, joys, and sorrows articulated.

Almost as important as the music, and sometimes more important, are the people that owned or worked in these stores. They are guides and gurus, the keepers of the culture, much of which without their knowledge would be inaccessible to so many. Folks who know what's happened, what's happening, and have an ear out for what is likely to happen.

I've been listening to music my whole life, and I have heard it pretty much every way you can imagine—from world-class recording studios to roadside shacks. On boomboxes and transistor radios, ridiculously over-priced home hi-fis' and old record players held together by dust. On the old school telephones (Anyone remember "dial a disc"?) to laptop computers. I've heard it played on 8-track cartridges, compact discs, and cassette tapes (prerecorded and homemade), and I have concluded that the all-round best way to go is a vinyl record played on a decent turntable.

And then there's the covers… Has there ever been a wrapper or box put around a commercially available product that had as much impact and influence as the long playing record sleeve? I still don't think so. A hopefully endless supply of visual stimulation, distractions galore, produced by all kinds of creative and/or crazed minds.

So it was a return to and improvement of the vinyl format that has led the way on this mission to ensure that the record store does not perish. It's easy for cynics to criticize and find fault, but what I have found so encouraging about Michael Kurtz and Carrie Colliton, who run Record Store Day here in the USA, is that their only agenda is to succeed in keeping independent record stores open and vinyl records available. Like any boots-on-the-ground operation, they learn and adapt as they go along, remaining true to their mission, but flexible in how to get it done. There's no blueprint for how to make what might appear to be a romantic notion into a reality. It requires a commitment to overcome more obstacles than they might have ever imagined. In recent years, I have met many store owners and staff who have assured me that without Record Store Day, their business would have folded, and so I give it both my full support and endorsement.

"Man does not live by bread alone" (to quote the Bible) and nor do many of us "live to work." I'm not suggesting that I can answer that "why are we all here" question, but I am suggesting that while we all are here, we listen to music. It's not the only thing to do, but it is one of the only things that can make most of whatever it is you are doing feel better.

—KOSMO VINYL (artist, cultural curator, enthusiast and
former consigliere to The Clash)
New York City
Edited by Christian Logan Wright

YEARS AGO, SOMEONE TOLD ME *that 1,200 high school kids were given a survey. A question was posed to them: Have you ever been to a standalone record shop? The number of kids that answered "yes" was...zero.*

Zero? How could that be possible? Then I got realistic and thought to myself, "Can you blame them?" How can record shops (or any shop for that matter) compete with Netflix, video games that take months to complete, cable, texting, the internet, etc.? Getting out of your chair at home to experience something in the real world has started to become a rare occurrence and, to a lot of people, an unnecessary one. Why go to a bookstore and get a real book? You can just download it. Why talk to other human beings, discuss different authors, writing styles, and influences? Just click your mouse. Well here's what they'll someday learn if they have a soul; there's no romance in a mouse click. There's no beauty in sitting for hours playing video games. The screen of an iPhone is convenient, but it's no comparison to a 70mm showing of a film in a gorgeous theater. The internet is two-dimensional...helpful and entertaining, but no replacement for face-to-face interaction with a human being. But we all know all of that, right? Well, do we? Maybe we know all that, but so what?

I think it's high time the mentors, big brothers, big sisters, parents, guardians, and neighborhood ne'er-do-wells start taking younger people that look up to them to a real record store and show them what an important part of life music really is. I trust no one who hasn't time for music. What a shame to leave a child, or worse, a generation orphaned from one of life's great beauties. And to the record stores, artists, labels, DJs, and journalists: we're all in this together. Show respect for the tangible music that you've dedicated your careers and lives to, and help it from becoming nothing more than disposable digital data.

Let's wake each other up.

The world hasn't stopped moving. Out there, people are still talking to each other face-to-face, exchanging ideas and turning each other on. Art houses are showing films, people are drinking coffee and telling tall tales, women and men are confusing each other, and record stores are selling discs full of soul that you haven't felt yet. So why do we choose to hide in our caves and settle for replication? We know better. We should. We need to reeducate ourselves about human interaction and the difference between downloading a track on a computer and talking to other people in person and getting turned onto music that you can hold in your hands and share with others. The size, shape, smell, texture, and sound of a vinyl record; how do you explain that to a teenager who doesn't know that it's a more beautiful musical experience than a mouse click? You get up off your ass, you grab them by the arm, and you take them there. You put the record in their hands. You make them drop the needle on the platter. Then they'll know.

Let's wake each other up.

As a Record Store Day (RSD) supporter, I'm proud to help in any way I can to invigorate whoever will listen with the idea that there is beauty and romance in the act of visiting a record shop and getting turned on to something new that could change the way they look at the world, other people, art, and ultimately, themselves.

Let's wake each other up.

—Jack White, 2013 Record Store Day Ambassador

CHAPTER ONE

The Report of My Death Was an Exaggeration

"I saw it dying. I saw it dead. And I saw it coming out of the grave, rising from the ashes..."
—Gerhard Blum, Sony Music Entertainment

[Vinyl emerges from oblivion, providing the most unlikely comeback story of the digital age.]

THE *BILLBOARD* HEADLINE ON MAY 11, 1991, screamed somewhat ominously, "The LP's Passage to Oblivion," announcing that the distribution companies owned by the major labels Warner/Elektra/Atlantic and Sony Music were no longer accepting returns from retailers on vinyl albums. Universal's distribution group wasn't either. Twenty years ago, six major record conglomerates (EMI, BMG, and Polygram since folded into three—Universal, Sony, and Warner) rode the compact disc (CD) as the cash-cow music format of choice. The internet, as a means of electronic distribution, still was a decade away from being a commercial option, playing catch-up from Napster's illicit wakeup call.

Looking back on the past three decades, two popular analog home entertainment formats (vinyl and cassette, which were actually the most popular formats in the late 1980s) were quickly replaced by supposed advanced digital technologies in fast succession (CD, digital downloads, and streaming). Then—no doubt thanks to Record Store Day's emergence in 2008—vinyl reemerges as a deluxe product where consumers are willing today to pay twice as much for a newly pressed vinyl LP than they did for a CD!?!

Did RSD's cofounders know for sure what they were doing? Of course not, and they were largely making it up as they went along. Record stores were selling mostly CDs in 2007 and some couldn't fathom stocking new vinyl once again in any kind of meaningful numbers, even though regular customers would always buy the three-dollar records in the used bins. But Michael Kurtz, who's become the face of the movement, and his band of RSD misfits persevered, mustering enough support to make a much bigger splash by 2009, only to continue to build year after year the monumental achievement that Record Store Day has become fifteen years later.

Record Store Day is a celebration of record stores—thus the "record store" in the name—but it is full of misconceptions, such as it was started as a ploy of the major labels, or the RSD cofounders and the record stores that sell the exclusive records all get rich off these limited editions, or RSD releases clog up the pressing plants so that other vinyl records can't get manufactured. All completely untrue.

Vinyl's rebirth in the digital age defies all economic, technological, and ecological logic. Firstly, it's expensive to manufacture an LP that, secondly, relies on mostly antique pressing equipment and processes, which largely haven't changed in a half century. And thirdly, records are made from polyvinyl (PVC), which is not the most green-friendly raw material, although today's pressing plants are far more conscious about sustainability than their 1970s counterparts, using modern processes and new equipment that reduce carbon emissions.

Record Store Day deserves substantial praise for kickstarting the entire vinyl supply chain, creating new opportunities for distribution companies, mastering and cutting facilities, raw material suppliers, packaging firms and printers, designers who create album graphics, turntable manufacturers, and ancillary products such as record sleeves and disc cleaning kits. It's no coincidence that vinyl's exponential growth year-to-year over the past fifteen years syncs up exactly with RSD's launch and the positive impact the 1,400 indie record stores feel in their communities.

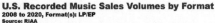

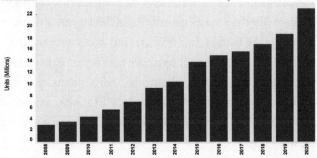

Speaking at the Making Vinyl conference in Hollywood in October 2019, David Bakula, senior vice president of Analytics, Insights, and Research for Nielsen Music/MRC Data, credited Record Store Day with "incredible foresight" to kickstart the vinyl comeback in 2008 when Bakula worked for a large distribution company. "After the [first] Record Store Day numbers came out, I went to my [boss] and said, 'I'm telling you, man, this vinyl thing, there's something here. This isn't just about Record Store Day. These numbers are overperforming every single week.' And he said to me, 'It's a rounding error, come back to me when it matters.' Well, it sure didn't take very long for it to matter."

By 2012, Nielsen reported vinyl represented 2.4 percent of the physical music business with 3.3 million units (with CDs accounting for the balance). In 2013, it grew to 3.5 percent of the physical business and 4.3 million units. In 2014, the jump went to 6.2 percent and 6.4 million units. In 2015, the steady growth went to 8.8 percent and 8.4 million units, followed by 11.2 percent and 9.5 million units in 2016. In 2017, the vinyl jump rose to 14 million units, and again in 2018 to more than 16 million units. In 2019 Bakula forecasted that vinyl was trending at 24 percent of the physical business. And in 2020, the Record Industry Association of America's (RIAA) reported that vinyl grew 28.7 percent to $626 million, which was more revenue that came in for CDs for the first time since 1986.

These numbers tell a positive story. But the problem is most record stores do not report their sales, so both Nielsen and RIAA estimate figures that unfortunately don't jibe with the large volumes pressing plants crank out these days or pumped through the retail supply chain. Yet the media's spread vinyl sales numbers that severely underestimate the market. In the US, record stores only buy titles that they are certain will be bought by music fans because they cannot be returned. Furthermore, only about 250 independent record stores in the United States report their sales to MRC Data, who clearly is estimating sales, since approximately 1,400 US stores participate in Record Store Day.

Sitting in the audience in the October 2018 Making Vinyl conference were representatives of the industry's leading pressing plants and distribution companies. When my PowerPoint presentation flashed an RIAA slide from two weeks earlier that reported 8.1 million vinyl units were sold in the first six months of that year, yells echoed throughout the ballroom that it was "way low." Afterward, Steve Sheldon, owner of the Rainbo, one of the world's largest vinyl pressing plants, said his California pressing plant at that point was cranking out 7 million units a year alone. United Record Pressing in Nashville, the nation's largest manufacturer, produced more LPs than Rainbo (which closed in January 2020 due to the high cost of doing business in California). Then there's additional output from twenty-seven other smaller US facilities, not to mention the sixty-three other plants around the world also making records, a good portion no doubt being imported for American consumers. Globally, 160 million records were pressed in 2021, estimated Making Vinyl.

Now put those numbers into perspective: Back in 2008 when Record Store Day launched, there were *only fourteen pressing plants in the United States and eight more elsewhere in the world for a total of twenty-two operated* with a last-man standing attitude. New operations sprung up during the past decade to meet the demand. But current pressing capacities globally add up to 160 million LPs a year, but demand by June 2021 required twice that amount, creating a backlog as much as ten months, *Billboard* reported.

Market research firm Deloitte nearly broke the internet in 2017 by estimating vinyl that year would be a $1 billion industry for the first time in decades. The firm took into account not only newly pressed vinyl, but also the sale of used records, turntables, and accessories. Since then, vinyl and ancillary revenue demonstrated, as of this writing, more than three years' worth of substantial growth. But Deloitte's Duncan Stewart, one of the 2017 report's two authors, won't quantify the market's current worth. "I can't just 'update' the number. Deloitte has rules and processes around this kind of thing," he says.

At Making Vinyl Virtual in December 2020, though, Stewart stated, "We think that the US number for [new vinyl sales] will be well over $500 million this year," partly based on flawed RIAA numbers, which "understate actual vinyl sales. They don't capture a lot of the small record shops; they don't capture sales of used vinyl. So the actual number, of course, would be even higher still."

However questionable RIAA's methodology might be, the organization's report for the first half of 2020 found vinyl album revenues of $232 million to comprise nearly two-thirds (62 percent) of total physical music revenues. That was quite a milestone, marking the first-time vinyl's dollar amounts exceeded that for CDs since the 1980s. (Interestingly, the report stated the volume of CD units still exceeded that of vinyl.)

Meanwhile, Deloitte's Stewart estimated in December 2020 that the US is 40 percent of the global vinyl market, which the firm in 2017 reported "came very close to a billion dollars [in 2017]... Our prediction came true." The researcher cited vinyl's "decent growth" in 2018 and 2019, and "a big jump even in the middle of a pandemic for 2020...Even post-pandemic, we'll be spending considerably more time at home. People are setting up their home offices, they are putting in sound systems, they are buying vinyl, and pulling vinyl out of storage."

Vinyl 2.0 is not your father's record business. New machinery suppliers have perfected nearly century-old processes with higher yields, sustainability, better-sounding, heavier, and creatively packaged records. "This is craftsman-level stuff," Jeff Truhn, operations manager of Cascade Record Pressing in Milwaukie, Oregon, told the Making Vinyl audience in 2018.

LPs produced for Record Store Day are pressed in fairly small quantities, which then creates a frenzy of consumer demand. Scores of people in any city where there's an RSD-participating record store line up the night before, in hopes of snaring a particular record, and often they walk out with many other impulse purchases not on their original list. So what if you're several hundred dollars poorer?

Today, consumers gladly shop at approximately 1,400 independent US record stores and another 3,000 doing business globally; Record Store Day is celebrated on every continent but Antarctica. While vinyl admittedly registered a negligible sales blip in the 1990s, the format never really went away, thanks to old-school DJs spinning dance records, audiophiles with their thousand-dollar-plus stereos supported by a few labels catering to that market, and flea-market crate diggers looking for collectibles. One person's trash is another's treasure, indeed. Those well-combed-over used record bins gave indie retailers confidence that perhaps vinyl still had some life in it.

Although Record Store Day exclusive releases are pressed in relatively low quantities of 15,000 or less, a non-RSD title like Jack White's 2014 solo record, *Lazaretto,* proved that a new, non-reissue album can sell 230,000 units on vinyl. Third Man Records head Ben Blackwell gave me the sales figure, as of March 2020. The Arctic Monkeys' *AM* was the second best-selling album on vinyl with 29,000 units that year. But the vinyl world was not nearly as large in 2014 as it is 2022. I have no doubt that a new album from Taylor Swift or Beyonce, who appeal to a younger demographic, could sell hundreds of thousands of copies in the new decade ahead.

Theory #1: The CD Made Vinyl's Comeback Possible

Isn't it interesting that *record* stores never ceased to be called "*record* stores" even when they were selling mostly compact discs? To understand why Vinyl 2.0 is working, we must hark back to the early 1980s when the industry replaced the LP with the shiny little disc known as the CD. As noted at the beginning of the chapter, retailers could return unsold CDs, which gave them an incentive to usher in a new format, but no longer would labels and distributors accept vinyl.

Nearly a quarter century later, when approached by the RSD cofounders about their vision, the major labels attached strings for the indie retailers and distributors if they were going to insist on bringing back vinyl: no returns, which is how they helped minimize vinyl's footprint and consumption in the early 1990s.

The carefree excesses of the 1970s and 1980s record business manifested itself in the adage "shipped platinum, returned gold" (signifying one million and 500,000 units, respectively) as a normal activity. The tongue-in-cheek, reverse version of the phrase smacks of the corrupt practices that resulted in prison sentences. Recommended reading for this insidious side of the industry that has since disappeared: *Stiffed—A True Story of MCA, the Music Business, and the Mafia* by William Knoedelseder (1993) and *Hit Men: Power Brokers and Fast Money Inside the Music Business* by Fredric Dannen (1990). Under such an environment, artists with gold records could find their supposed best-sellers in the cut-out bins, while owing their labels ridiculous amounts of money for video production costs.

The major labels' ulterior motive in the 1980s: Make sure that CDs reinvigorated the industry at a time videogames and VHS captured a commanding share of the home entertainment market, as did MTV on cable TV. The record industry needed to reinvent itself and make itself relevant again. Portable cassette players gave music lovers the soundtrack of their minds as they walked about the street or daydreamed on a mass-transit commute. In fact, RIAA data shows *cassettes from 1983 until 1990 were the most popular prerecorded music format*, as tape decks were standard car accessories. As CDs gained acceptance, portable disc players improved on the tape variety and in-dash CD players became standard automobile features.

Launched commercially in 1982, the CD quickly gained traction as the labels and retail supported the format, most importantly by accepting returns. By 1986, 45 million discs were produced, exceeding the number of LPs. Two years later, more than twice the number of CDs (149.7 million) were shipped than LPs (72.4 million). In 1990, worldwide CD sales hit 288 million discs, even with CD player penetration in only 28 percent of US households.

In 2000, the CD peaked by selling 785 million units in the US; in 2018, that total plummeted to about 70 million units. In 2001, CDs represented 91 percent of US music units shipped, reported the RIAA. In 2002, CD's twentieth anniversary, 1.63 billion audio discs were replicated, reported the International Recording Media Association. And then the CD ceiling started to cave, partly because in 1999 Napster and other "peer-to-peer" file-sharing services unleashed the concept of free illegal music, and partly because they were overpriced. From a manufacturing standpoint, the CD became a mass-produced commodity. The best-selling CD soon became a blank CD-R, as optical drives became standard in laptops and Apple legitimized paid downloadable music with its easily navigated iTunes library and well-designed iPod where earlier MP3 players appeared clumsy.

CDs ruled for at least twenty-five years. Yet even when record stores stopped carrying *vinyl*—the word always seemed synonymous with *record*—customers didn't say they were going to the CD store. Perhaps a case in semantics, but the technical term for a physical carrier of music is "phonorecord." The only people who hear of a phonorecord are music lawyers who chase down royalties.

Theory #2: Limited-Editions Worked

Record Store Day's cofounders had the right idea. Throw a party and create limited edition releases. If they kept production levels down, the better chance music fans would get excited about collecting limited editions of releases that have a very good chance of selling out forever if you don't make it to the store that special day in April and on Black Friday. You snooze you lose, or risk collectors paying a ransom online, just like fans of everything from designer sneakers to luxury automobiles do. But how do you create this level of excitement without having greedy speculators ruin the fun?

What irks Record Store Day participants most is when speculators try to greedily capitalize on a good thing by posting RSD releases at jacked-up prices months before they're available, as if they have them in their possession, which is impossible. RSD holds its participating stores to a "pledge" that they only sell the exclusive releases at the established price, or risk not being labeled an official Record Store Day retailer. But generally, the limited-edition system works fine for both stores and fans.

As you delve into the Record Store Day world, you get a feeling from Kurtz and RSD cofounder Carrie Colliton—who manage RSD on a daily basis in consultation with others—that they might just be making it up as they go along. Such a loose approach to act on a hunch and envision the possibilities is certainly a refreshing departure from the corporate world. But they also don't rest on laurels, always trying new approaches to widening the appeal of Record Store Day.

Fifteen years ago, we coped without smartphones being at the center of our daily existence, and the notion of having instantaneous access to the world's recorded output for a fairly nominal subscription fee seemed like pie in the sky. Consider the convenience that digital music subscriptions—and the promise of the celestial jukebox in the sky—provided as mobile phones soon became the center of entertainment in the palm of your hand.

But a digital file is "a crappy gift," as pioneer rap label Tommy Boy, head Tom Silverman, quipped in 2015 at his New Music Seminar conference, compared to the permanence of a 12-inch x 12-inch physical object of beauty, even before it's placed on a turntable. No wonder many purchasers never listen and just hang the cover on the wall. However, to do so is near blasphemy. As vinyl evangelist Jack White insists, "Your turntable is not dead." And even if it is, there are plenty of new options to spin your records from under a hundred dollars to a million dollar audiophile setup.

A Record Production Primer

To understand the current vinyl revival, one must learn a little technological history. Inventors Thomas Edison and Emile Berliner were tinkering with capturing and playing back sound since the late 1870s. Their approaches and aims were different. Edison, an American, built a tinfoil-wrapped cylinder, which he viewed as a dictation machine for the office. German expat Berliner, on the other hand, conceived immediately recorded music on a disk sitting on a primitive turntable, equipped with a stylus. Ten years after Edison's "phonograph," Berliner filed his patent for his hand-cranked "Gramophone," marking the first format war, an antecedent to the mid-1970s videocassette wars of Beta vs. VHS, or the early 2000's feud over Super Audio CD vs. DVD-Audio. When it comes to consumer electronics, coexistence rarely works, perhaps prerecorded 8-track tapes and audiocassettes during the go-go years of the 1970s being the exception.

Edison's cylinders hit their sales peak in 1907. By 1912, Edison realized the Berliner model was winning the war, and he introduced disc phonographs, although still producing the cylinders until 1929. Berliner's machine required a stylus to cut a groove for capture and playback on a chemically treated material on a round, flat disc. Berliner gained investment from US corporate backers for his vertically integrated operation, signing up talent, such as the opera singer Caruso. Edison eventually rethought his business model, and licensed music for his cylinders and…round discs. Berliner's records were conceived with mass production in mind. From the cut master disc, a stamper was made, conceptually no different from today's vinyl-making process. Playing time generally was under five minutes, and a two-sided disc soon emerged. Edison halted production of his records and record players because of the Depression. With such a global economic crisis, only the well-to-do could afford such a home luxury. Records spinning at 78-rpm in diameter sizes from five to fourteen inches were made out of easy breakable shellac, which was replaced in the 1940s by polyvinyl chloride (PVC), which we now refer to as simply "vinyl." The plastic's manufacturing advantages included stability, durability, inexpensive, easily formed and molded. In development for about a decade, World War II led CBS to delay its introduction of a new long-playing "LP" offering up to fifteen minutes of music per side until 1948.

Soon thereafter, RCA debuted its seven-inch "singles" spun at 45 rpm, clearly aimed at the bar jukebox and youth markets. Enter Elvis Presley in the 1950s, the Beatles, British Invasion, Motown, and all the Top 40 hits of the 1960s on both sides of the Atlantic emanating from transistor AM radios. Kids soon had their own portable record players to play the relatively inexpensive 45s—affordable with allowance money—in the privacy of their homes. (Record Store Day has brought back the seven-inch singles market as well, and every year features an array of coveted collectibles.) Since the 1950s, stereo pioneers experimented with putting two channels into a single record groove. By the mid-1960s and the rise of FM radio, they perfected the sound, resulting in record labels' focus on long-playing albums or LPs.

An irony of the vinyl comeback is purists coveting recordings of the Beatles and the Rolling Stones in mono instead of stereo, and it's no accident that often a RSD release's selling point is "now in mono."

Personally speaking, why would you want to hear *Sgt. Pepper's Lonely Hearts Club Band* or *Their Satanic Majesties Request* in anything but stereo? In fact, I wouldn't mind bringing back Quadraphonic; I'm all in favor of accommodating choice.

Remastered mono vinyl was at the center of the strategy of Sundazed Records, a reissue label specializing in lost classics from the 1960s, founded by Bob Irwin in 1989. Previously a reissue producer for Sony Music, Irwin enjoyed an inside track on the vinyl comeback by being able to license Byrds and Bob Dylan because the major had no interest at the time in bringing back the format to a niche audience. Irwin told me in November 2002 for *Medialine* magazine, which I edited at the time:

> "I don't feel that anybody making vinyl has to plead their case. All any average Joe has to do is flip on their tube on a weekday night for three hours during primetime, and you're going to see at least one commercial romanticizing vinyl or a big-ass rack of records. It's the truth. I've seen it everywhere from Mohawk Carpeting to Tide detergent to Volkswagen."

Fast forward a few years. Even to the casual observer, 2006 sucked—well, maybe not as bad as 2020. It didn't bode well for the future of brick-and-mortar retail selling home entertainment via physical media (i.e., CD and vinyl on life support; DVDs would suffer that fate a few years later when streaming movies became more popular than watching on an optical disc). EMI Music chairman and chief executive, Alain Levy, told a London Business School audience in 2006 that the CD was "dead." Such a proclamation surely made independent music shops grimace because they were still selling healthy volumes of new and used CDs. (Used because consumers were increasingly dumping their collections as they digitized them onto their laptops, which now also held their iTunes purchases of single songs for 99 cents and full albums at $9.99. Apple Computer and their stockholders became richer.)

On Decemeber 22, 2006, Tower Records liquidated and closed permanently its remaining eighty-nine US stores (from nearly 200 stores in twenty-one states with $1 billion in revenue at its peak), marking the end of an era as far as a music-oriented "megastore" chain succeeding in the digital age. Tower's demise came on the heels of HMV in 2004 pulling out of the US market after a decade of its superstores losing money (£1 million in 2004). Virgin by 2009 liquidated its twenty-three US stores, which had generated a peak annual revenue of $310 million. But along with Tower, HMV, and Virgin going defunct, mall-based corporate chains with smaller record stores also went belly-up, including Sam Goody, Strawberries, Coconuts, Peaches, Tape World, Camelot, Turtle's, and National Record Mart. Also biting the dust during this period were national chain Circuit City (2009) and regional chain The Wiz (2003), both specializing in electronics and appliances with new CDs priced at $9.99 retail as "loss leaders" below wholesale to get consumers to purchase big-ticket items, also bit the dust.

For the independent record stores managing to hold on, the behemoths' disappearance could mean one of two things: 1) physical media was doomed, or 2) an opportunity was knocking on the door. Some diversified into other product lines, such as DVDs, T-shirts, and comic books, but other merchandise didn't save the big chains. In 2007, the record industry needed to be convinced that vinyl remained a viable product. Could it be a unifying campaign that celebrates record stores as a cultural phenomenon where people learn about life, meet future spouses, and get enriched with great music that otherwise would be left unheard? You know, something like Record Store Day.

The RSD story is an elixir of community, business, art, music, and records. The secret sauce is the entrepreneurs behind the stores themselves and people who work there, those who upon reaching adulthood decided to "not get a real job," or after getting a taste of corporate America (or anywhere else) decided it's not for them.

It's no wonder so many A-list musicians who worked in record stores include the likes of Guns 'n' Roses' Axl Rose and Slash, who were Tower Records employees. Slash, in fact, was arrested for shoplifting from the same Sunset Boulevard store that he was supposedly banned from. Axl managed Tower Video across the street. R.E.M. guitarist Peter Buck met his future lead singer Michael Stipe at the record store where he worked. Similarly, Hüsker Dü's Bob Mould met the band's future bassist Grant Hart while Hart was working at a St. Paul record store; their drummer Greg Norton worked at a different store. Other record store employees include future RSD ambassadors Iggy Pop and Dave Grohl, as well as Motley Crue's Nikki Sixx, Joy Division's Ian Curtis, Moby, and Nelly Furtado.

Another former record store clerk Jeff Tweedy, who also found his face on record jackets, worked at Euclid Records in St. Louis before making it with Uncle Tupelo and then Wilco. Not surprisingly, those bands' archival music is often on sale for RSD. In fact, a 1994 Uncle Tupelo live show became an RSD live album in 2020.

Not surprisingly, Tweedy these days—often on Record Store Day—does in-store appearances or performances. Paramore, Ani DiFranco, Common, Steve Earle, Panic! At the Disco, Regina Spektor, Dresden Dolls, Marshall Crenshaw, among numerous others, typically plan indie-store RSD stops whenever they're on tour both domestically and overseas. Some still record for major record labels and others have gone the indie route. In Record Store Day's early years, with the exception of the Warner Music Group, the major labels didn't take seriously the new business models floated by RSD's cofounders.

"Early on in the vinyl resurgence, many in the industry dismissed the trend as a niche format," admits Sujata Murthy, Universal Music Enterprises' senior vice president of media and artists and repertoire. "In recent years, no further convincing is necessary of artists or the industry as commercial viability is well established, while vinyl continues to outperform expectations year over year," she adds, crediting RSD and indie stores being at the forefront of vinyl's resurgence fifteen years ago.

Gerhard Blum, Sony Music Entertainment's senior vice president, distribution and supply chain international, comments that typically a major label requires four years to respond to a music industry trend, so the slow enthusiasm for Record Store Day is not surprising, and he remains astounded by the format's resurrection.

"I saw it dying. I saw it dead. And I saw it coming out of the grave, rising from the ashes, like the whole Phoenix cycle, you could say. No one in the industry can get enough vinyl right now. This is beyond your wildest dreams. The independent sector—the stores and Record Store Day—can claim that they basically ensured the resurrection or the survival of the vinyl format."

CHAPTER TWO

Noise in the Basement

*"Filling a terabit storage device with ten thousand music files isn't any-
where as engaging as wandering through a great record store."*
—Fred Goodman, *Fortune's Fool* (2010)

*[2005–2007: In the wake of Tower Records' demise, independent record
stores contemplate their collective futures and conceive Record Store Day.]*

ON AUGUST 5, 2002, SIX years prior to steering the first Record Store
Day, the coalition of independent record stores called the Music
Monitor Network held a convention in New York City. Sam Phillips,
the owner of the pioneering Sun Records label and recording studio,
was the keynote speaker. The seventy-nine-year-old Phillips certainly
knew his audience.

> "I have been in the music business all my life just about,
> and I can truly say that there are no greater people on the
> face of God's earth than the independent retail/record
> merchandiser...I don't think Elvis [Presley] would have
> made it had it not been for individual stores, and independent
> distributors...There would be no Elvis. There would be no
> Johnny Cash. There'd be no B. B. King. There'd be no Carl
> Perkins. There would be no Jerry Lee Lewis. There would
> be no Roy Orbison...We owe all of that to the independents
> and the independent people that work so hard for us to have
> something that could be accepted through their efforts,

hard work, and desire to keep a personal feeling in every record, no matter how many thousands, or hundreds of thousands, of records you might sell in a year. Your business is very intimate to your soul and the way you feel. It's not just another business."

Phillips implored the store owners, who he called "the bravest and smartest," to keep the faith. "I know what you are confronted with." What he was alluding to was the behemoth music chains' unfair advantage that included them receiving volume breaks not offered to independent record stores. Furthermore, some "big box" retailers, as a corporate strategy, were selling CDs at a loss so music fans buy other merchandise.

"I have nothing against big business, but when it comes to the ideal of something as intimate as music, something that has changed the face of this earth for better, made us all understand each other better…to think that the United States could live without you people, it makes me want to cry."

The man who gave Elvis his big break sadly passed away less than a year later. He certainly could have been talking about Record Store Day's cofounders and everyone who has contributed to vinyl's nearly unbelievable resurgence when he said, "I know that there is nobody more tenacious in the business than the individual thinker, the individual worker, known as the individual merchandiser of music."

The Folks Behind RSD

Carrie Colliton is an army brat—something she shares with Michael Kurtz. "I grew up all over the place. I went to college at Virginia Tech in Blacksburg, Virginia, where there were several record stores." Among them was The Record Exchange, which operated seven stores in Virginia and North Carolina in the early 1990s.

Kurtz handled the chain's marketing. Carrie worked in one of the stores. "My very first phone conversation with Michael was calling him as a very excited staff member, saying: 'Hey, the Lemonheads are coming to town, and I'd like to do a contest with them to do an in-store' [performance/signing]." Kurtz remembers the event pretty well, "Carrie was a Lemonheads fan and wanted to do this signing with the band. What I discovered later was Evan Dando came to the record store, got really stoned, and had reservations about doing the signing for a record store full of fans excited to meet him. It was Carrie who convinced him to do it. In the end, Evan and hundreds of Lemonheads' fans were happy. Seeing Carrie handle that tricky situation gave me early confidence in working with her."

The Record Exchange had a track record of mounting successful in-store promotions at all of its stores and, at its peak, hosted more than 400 artist appearances in just one year. The chain's stores knew how to throw a party, but the Blacksburg store's isolation in the mountains particularly required the locals "to make our own fun," Colliton remembers. Situated between Washington, DC, and Chapel Hill, North Carolina, Blacksburg presented the perfect tour stop "because they had to spend the night somewhere…We would book shows just because we wanted to bring in on-the-verge bands like Uncle Tupelo, who would play because we could feed them at a potluck and put them up ourselves." The record stores played a big part in Blacksburg creating its own scene. "That was like a snow globe in my life. I enjoyed that part of my life so much," she added. As the chain grew, Carrie graduated and was ready to leave the college town. She helped open a new location of The Record Exchange in Chapel Hill, where Kurtz was located, and subsequently worked in the Raleigh store. From there, "I met [Michael] in person and started doing marketing for the whole chain. Eventually he got promoted, and I got promoted as his assistant."

The Record Exchange published an in-house magazine called *The Music Monitor*, created by Charlie Johnson, that served as a catalyst for an indie-store coalition to be known as the Music Monitor Network. The Record Exchange grew to thirteen stores, then aligned with a twenty-two-store chain called Cats Music in Tennessee and South Carolina, along with The Gallery of Sound, an eight-store chain in Pennsylvania, all of which carried the magazine. At its height, the Music Monitor Network would represent ten independently-owned chains across the United States, and The Music Monitor would have a circulation of 250,000. Eventually, Kurtz left The Record Exchange to run the coalition full-time, and Colliton took Michael's job.

> Remembers Carrie: "There were a lot of women running The Record Exchange. That was really impressive for the time, especially as I grew to know more about the industry. Our buyer, marketing, HR, operations, and maybe one other position were all women. In the nineties for a record store chain, that's pretty great." Looking back on her working relationship with Kurtz, Colliton recognizes that typically "what would happen is [Kurtz] would form an idea and I would work with him on it, on the details of getting it done, until we were running the coalition together, which is now going strong as The Dept. of Record Stores, and the two of us now do that with Record Store Day as well, along with the two other independent record store coalitions."

The other coalitions are the Coalition of Independent Music Stores (CIMS), consisting mostly single-location iconic record stores spread across the country, and The Alliance of Independent Media Stores (AIMS).

The owners of stores in these coalitions were competitive with each other—within and across coalitions, especially when there was more than one coalition represented in a market, but also generally cut from the same cloth. What they had in common—selling music from brick-and-mortar stores in the digital age and authentically connecting with their favorite artists—outweighed any relatively minor differences. (Collectively, the coalitions still represent only a small number of the approximately 1,400 stores that currently participate in Record Store Day.)

In 2005, CIMS founder Don VanCleave launched an independent distribution company called Junketboy, and worked with Kurtz to create exclusive CDs for indie record stores. VanCleave recalls the catalyst:

> "In the late 1990s, record stores were really getting inundated with customers asking about whether they had in stock the CDs that some of the big box retail chains were selling. They were exclusive titles with additional content like an extra disc containing a concert, extra songs, or outtakes. CIMS members were outraged; our customers always bought those artists from us, and felt our offerings were inferior to what Target or Best Buy were selling. Theirs would have an extra disc with exclusive content—interesting things that people who shopped at our stores wanted. It put us in an unfair position. And then to add insult to injury, a lot of times those products at the chain stores with extra content would also be priced below our costs."

That retail "loss-leader" strategy also created a scenario wherein it was cheaper for record stores to buy CDs from mass merchants than it was directly from the majors. The indie record store coalitions raised hell about the issue at the convention of the National Association of Recording Merchandisers (NARM), now known as Music Biz, which had been dominated by the big chains like Tower Records. VanCleave and Kurtz told the major labels they were overlooking the huge sales base that independent stores collectively represented. Interscope's Christina Meloche worked with Kurtz and VanCleave to create the *Weezer Live in Japan* CD. VanCleave explains.

"We sold 25,000 copies of that CD in a week. We were off to the races getting exclusives. It kind of dawned on us that there are a lot of bands out there selling CDs direct to fans, on their web stores, at their shows, and a lot of content like that laying around. So, we started buying a lot of shows directly from Phish, for example, and distributing those into indie record stores. So, we started a distribution company to start handling that stuff."

Junketboy morphed into what's now known as ThinkIndie.com, which has also released exclusive albums for independent record stores by Pearl Jam, John Mayer, Deathcab for Cutie, Jack Johnson, Kings of Leon, My Morning Jacket, Bright Eyes, among others.

Simultaneous to the creation of ThinkIndie, the Department of Record Stores launched a "creative conference" in September 2006 in Raleigh, North Carolina, inside SPARKcon, the brainchild of cellist/product engineer Aly Khalifa. Of a similar mindset, Kurtz naturally connected with Khalifa.

"Aly's idea was to bring together various people to discuss creative ideas that would leapfrog an industry forward. I worked with Aly first as a musician in the band Semicolon, which was on the Shimmydisc label, and on a project we called Facepod back in 2005. The idea for the Facepod was to create an accessory for iPods that you could hang around your neck with a lanyard or set up on your desk so that you could view the screen. Various record labels supported us by creating lanyards for artists as diverse as Green Day and Little Brother. The idea was that fans would buy the artist's new album at a record store and get this fan piece. At the time, I was living in NYC and people were really adopting the iPod. I could see the technological wave coming so why not get in front of it and create an iPod accessory only available at record stores for free with the purchase of an album. Unfortunately, at the time, and outside of New York City, almost no one had adopted the iPod yet so they went out to stores only to be greeted by a lot of head scratching. We did get the attention of Apple though, and they sent us a cease-and-desist letter and that was the end of the Facepod."

Kurtz worked on the music panels of SPARKcon, which was attended by various music industry people, including Mike Doernberg, cofounder/CEO of the fledgling social media site ReverbNation, a platform founded in 2006 for independent musicians, producers, and venues to collaborate and communicate. Sessions tackled how to make record stores relevant in the rapidly developing online world. The record store leaders realized they needed to get together again the next year for another big meeting to build on what was discussed at SPARKcon. And they'd need to bring together even more record stores. Bryan Burkert, owner of the Baltimore and Syracuse record stores The Sound Garden, volunteered to host the next year in Baltimore, at a new event he dubbed "Noise in the Basement." As part of his pitch, he expressed strongly that the coalitions needed to "stop having meetings in hotels next to airports."

> "Record store owners, the label people, and everybody come in and are just miserable watching industry promotion 'sizzle reels' made for Walmart. Fells Point is a historic party district, and I wanted everybody to come to celebrate record stores. It would enable all the labels and distributors to have nights with live bands at the Fletcher's night club and at The Sound Garden, my record store. If we did that, we would take it back to our roots and have some fun."

By mid-2007, Michael Kurtz was toying with the possibility of getting the US Post Office to issue a postage stamp commemorating indie record stores, which would then spur live performances and special releases on a single day. Kurtz coined the concept

"Indie Record Store Day," and in late July, ran the idea by Chris Brown, with the Maine-based record store chain Bull Moose Music.

Brown replied in an email to an earlier conversation he'd had with Kurtz about "Indie Record Store Day," asking whether he was familiar with Free Comic Book Day, a successful comic bookstore promotion, started in 2002. Brown suggested they should publish a comic book with a record store theme and sell it at record stores. He went on to say that they should explore "Indie Record Store Day" later, proposing that it be a national event, with licensed pieces, promotional CDs, and special events in stores. The coalitions had already been creating promotional CDs, licensed records, and special events, so Kurtz decided it made sense to allot thirty minutes at the upcoming Baltimore get-together to map out everyone's ideas about what would become Record Store Day, since members of all three record store coalitions—CIMS, Music Monitor, and AIMS, as well as northeastern chain Newbury Comics—were planning to be at Noise in the Basement. The most important of which would be the idea of resurrecting vinyl.

AIMS head Eric Levin also owns the successful Atlanta store Criminal Records, a record store and comic book hub in Atlanta. His store had been part of Free Comic Book Day, and he told Kurtz they should consider something similar but with a major difference: stores would sell newly pressed vinyl. Levin's own customers were buying his store's used vinyl, and he was convinced they would be enthusiastic for new records not available anywhere else. Kurtz admits he was somewhat skeptical because it was "at a time when almost nobody was carrying new vinyl." A few store owners he queried replied tersely, "What? We sell CDs."

At Noise in the Basement, Kurtz planned to relay Chris and Eric's ideas, and the concept of borrowing from Free Comic Book Day but emphasizing their event would be a celebration of record store culture, not a day to simply give away what they normally sold. Colliton explains the difference:

"Our idea was a celebration of the store, whereas Free Comic Book Day is a celebration of the actual artifact, the comic book—and secondarily the stores that sell them. But the draw is primarily getting a free, collectible comic book. That was a pretty big distinction we made from the beginning. To this day, what people still get most confused about is that Record Store Day is not about a format. We're not Vinyl Day, CD Day, or Cassette Day…We're Record Store Day, those four physical walls, and the people and things inside them. At Noise in the Basement, our stores were coming together for a big meeting to figure out how to celebrate that. Clearly the media and the public didn't realize many stores were doing very well. So every store should throw a party on Record Store Day, invite the local press and show them the record store is part of your community all year long. Fans listen, learn about and buy music there, and meet artists at the in-store appearances. Record Store Day should be a celebration of all of that and of the people who work there, the customers who shop there, and the musicians who make the music that is sold there."

RSD idea left for last in Baltimore

The Baltimore meeting schedule was packed during the week, Kurtz remembers:

"We talked about music, what was happening at the stores and record labels brought in artists to come meet and play music for us. The then relatively unknown Avett Brothers performed and met with us in the record store. Regina Spektor, Atmosphere & Brother Ali, Josh Ritter, Aesop Rock, Raheem DeVaughn, and Flyleaf performed. Vintage Vinyl's Rob introduced an eighteen-year-old artist he was passionate about by the name of Laura Marling, and she performed with just an acoustic guitar, just before cast members of the TV series *The Wire* walked in to hang and talk with us about making the series in Baltimore."

Kurtz remembers toward the end of the event trying to get people to stick around and talk about this idea called "Indie Record Store Day."

The discussion that led to the creation of Record Store Day took place on the morning of September 22, 2007, literally closing out Noise in the Basement, as people were checking out of their hotels and getting ready to hit the airport. Less than ten people were present. No one recognized they would be creating the largest single-day music event in the world, one that would lead to the most improbable technological comeback of the twenty-first century. However, they had plenty of questions, and more of those would come: What did it take to make such an event happen and bring back vinyl? Who would be involved? Must it be backed by major corporations? How do they fend off incorrect theories that it would turn into a ploy to make a lot of money for the organizers, as some online trolls suggest?

After the final night of partying, most of the attendees were checking out of the hotel. Kurtz and Levin tried to round up the stragglers for one more impromptu final meeting. Burkert is not sure if he was present at the pivotal Saturday morning coffee shop when everyone present agreed on doing RSD, "but I definitely was in Broadway Square when the idea was broached." Kurtz remembers Levin being at the coffee shop and "essential" to the RSD story because "Eric really pushed the concept of vinyl."

Dilyn Radakovitz, whose Northern California chain Dimple closed in 2019, also remembers Levin being there and recalls the scene vividly.

"We were all hungover [due to partying the night before at Burkert's club]. Some people were waiting for cabs to leave the hotel and go back to the airport. A stack of newspapers was plunked down where they were hanging out, drinking coffee at the Admiral Fell Inn lobby with an ominous front-page headline something like: TOWER RECORDS CLOSED FOR GOOD. And we all looked at each other, thinking, 'Uh oh.' I was friendly with Russ [Solomon, Tower's owner and CEO]. We sat there. We knew [Tower] was in trouble for a long time, but we just kept thinking in our own little world that the record labels would just keep saving them. Most of the top people at the labels had all been employees of Russ's at one time or another. So we couldn't even imagine them not helping him. We knew immediately that if Tower goes—even though they were taking up so much of the advertising dollars and everything—that means all the labels were going to downsize. You're not going to have a sales rep in every market anymore."

Fourteen years later, Levin can't really tell the story of the Baltimore meeting when Record Store Day was decided.

"My recollection is not there. This is where I get really foggy, because I was traveling so much for the AIMS coalition, our own meetings, visiting stores to vet them for membership, going to New York and Los Angeles several times a year. None of that was on my life schedule. I've never thought I'd be a suitcase guy."

Current CIMS general manager Andrea Paschal, who worked in record stores since college, also can't picture in her mind what actually happened at the Noise in the Basement.

"I'll be honest, my memories are pretty fuzzy. There definitely were a lot of people who were crucial in helping [the Record Store Day] idea to grow. The biggest thing that I remember about it is we were working with Michael Kurtz, who was working to put together promotions across the coalitions. Cool promotional stuff for the stores."

Chris Brown couldn't stay to hear passionate Levin's pitch for everyone to focus on selling new vinyl or help Kurtz roundup support for the campaign. "I left early because I knew Michael had it well under control," Brown explains, adding that Kurtz is "really good at communicating [to others]."

However, Stephanie Huff, was present, representing The Exclusive Company, a Wisconsin-based record store chain that began in 1956; she became its general manager in 2001. She especially remembers what was discussed at the breakfast meeting:

"I remember the night before we were in this dank, dark bar watching bands. The next morning was the day everybody was flying home. And Michael [Kurtz] is like, 'Whoever can stick around, come to this meeting, and hear me out. I think I've got something here that might be really good.' So, we all met at the coffee shop. Michael and Eric Levin were the ones addressing this very small group, maybe seven or eight people. There weren't that many people who were able to stick around. We were always looking for something [that would help business]. Vinyl had not yet made the resurgence that it ended up becoming. This was a period of segmentation for record stores. It was announced that weekend Tower Records was closing permanently. So many articles at that time were just doom and gloom, 'How is the record store going to survive?' The big story was always digital downloads, and albums were starting to get released digitally before they were physically. That's the setting and what we were dealing with. I knew Eric and Michael had been talking about it prior to this meeting. Eric's record store in Atlanta also sold comic books. He said, 'Every year, they have Free Comic Book Day, and it's a big celebration.

They give away comics, and publish collectibles, numbered pieces, exclusives, just for comic book stores that day.' At first, I thought, 'Okay, I guess we can do that. That would be fun. Let's see if we can make something happen.'"

Huff knew The Exclusive Company's owner, James A. Giombetti, who goes by "Mr. G," would be interested in the concept because of the exclusivity angle. Afterall, it's in the company's name.

"[Mr. G] was always talking about exclusivity, and felt the CD was over-commoditized. It was just everywhere, Best Buy, Walmart, Target, there were just too many players. And so when I heard 'exclusives' I got a little excited because we can make something happen with that."

Kurtz and Colliton believed that Amy Dorfman of Newbury Comics was at the meeting where Record Store Day hatched. Amy remembers otherwise. "I was there [in Baltimore] at the time, but I wasn't at that meeting." As it turns out, her Newbury colleague and buyer Larry Mansdorf was indeed representing the chain at that pivotal moment. "Yes, in theory, I was [at the coffee shop meeting] from what I recall," responds Mansdorf, participating in the same Zoom call with the author and Dorfman. After the Noise in the Basement, Dorfman joined the group charged with getting Record Store Day off the ground instead of Mansdorf because Newbury owner Mike Dreese "thought it was more of a marketing job."

Burkert considered the four days of Noise a major success, and strongly felt the coalitions needed to maximize the support from artists and their management. The entrepreneur in him recognized the ecosystem that provides his store with merchandise.

"Labels and distributors had nights with live bands and invited all record store owners to attend. It was a true celebration of music, record stores, and record store culture, with all these record store owners from all over the country hanging out and partying with the label people and artists.

We got back to our roots of who and what were. Physical products take a lot more hands to operate. But it was the artists' desire to have physical products that really helped us. The artists were more into keeping us around than I felt the [then] current state of some of the majors (labels). I won't say the same about the indie labels; they really relied on us for a bulk of their sales. They also know how to have fun."

So no one person was responsible for creating Record Store Day? Cofounder Colliton explains:

"It's kind of cool that Record Store Day is claimed by a bunch of people. Michael [Kurtz] has always said Record Store Day is an open-source event because in order for it to work, everybody anywhere along the line has to have some sort of ownership in it. You have to feel like it's your thing in order for it to work because there's a lot of extra work that goes into it. And it can be very frustrating. But everybody loves it because they feel like 'this is mine. This is my thing. I want to nurture it and let it grow.' The origin story of Record Store Day is kind of like that."

To illustrate the point, when asked who invented Record Store Day, Kurtz simply said with a chuckle, "Well, my favorite version of who invented Record Store Day came from Twist & Shout's Paul Epstein. At one point in an interview for a local Denver publication, Paul said, 'Michael and I came up with the idea for Record Store Day while smoking pot in a hotel room.'"

In the end, Radakovitz says that Kurtz was picked to lead the Record Store Day charge because of his congenial personality and ability to get along with everybody (including Paul Epstein). Still Kurtz required like-minded, persuasive individuals to rally support.

How the name "Record Store Day" Was Chosen

In the original discussion between Kurtz and Brown, Kurtz referred to an event called "Indie Record Store Day," Michael remembers.

> "It was really just a placeholder name for a period of time but with continued discussions, it became clear that people understood what you meant when you said 'record store' and that gave the name Record Store Day weight to me. I went through a process of talking to different people, mainly record store owners. We kicked around different names. There was a dispute about [being known as] record stores because a lot of them were selling not only music but also movies on DVDs, pop-culture merchandise, and all that kind of stuff. In the end, based on all the feedback, we went with Record Store Day. I took the heat with people who didn't like it, who were unhappy about it because they felt like it was too limiting. I saw a bigger meaning to it, almost like a community kind of thing, like a church."

The next hurdles would be timing and the focus on vinyl records, Kurtz realized.

> "Once Easter arrives, April is pretty open. There's not a lot of music industry activity happening or a lot of releases coming out. So it became apparent that it would really help the stores to do it in late spring since it's before the summer tours start. People vacation in the summer, so that was no good. Carrie examined twenty-seven other holidays, and we discussed schedules with store owners and their priorities. A lot of them said, 'Hey, my kids get out of school in June,' so that didn't make sense. And you can't do it too close to the end of the year, because there's already a holiday season then. I don't think the stores wanted it to be in the summer, and we definitely wouldn't want it to be right in the middle of the

fourth quarter. I think we were trying to stimulate business at another time of the year that's not Christmas. But that's not the summertime either. So April seemed like the right fit. Carrie and I narrowed it down to the third Saturday in April."

Once the Noise in the Basement crew approved the Record Store Day concept, pushing the vinyl concept to the industry at large wasn't an easy sale, remembers Radakovitz, mainly because of the razor-thin margins for LPs that they can't return if they didn't sell.

"You don't really make money on new vinyl. If you're lucky, you're working on maybe margins of 23 to 25 percent if it's punk or metal, the underground stuff. But on the brand new, regular (i.e., most popular) stuff that you're going to sell a ton of, you're probably only using 15 to 17 percent you're making, and it's costing a lot to bring in."

Bringing in exclusive products that music fans can't buy elsewhere was important to the Record Store Day concept, but so was emphasizing what record stores bring to their local communities, which is why Newbury Comics wanted to be involved in the RSD effort, remembers Dorfman.

"For us, Record Store Day at the beginning was more about just celebrating record stores. We planned events at all of our stores, just like parties; we would have food, we would have all kinds of things, we would have record radio stations broadcasting live celebrating record stores."

The executive committee formed around implementing Record Store Day, composed of Kurtz, Levin, VanCleave, Colliton, and Dorfman, spoke often after the Baltimore meeting, but a face-to-face was necessary early in the new year, remembers Michael.

"We all met in New York City on January 17, 2008, for what we called the 'Indie Super Pow-Wow Meeting,' at which it was determined that Record Store Day would launch on Saturday, April 18, 2008, and would occur on every third Saturday in April going forward with Kurtz reaching out to artists through their labels to see if they would provide a quote about their thoughts on record stores. A goal was set to get vinyl records made, artist events happening, and to get 200 record stores (that goal was exceeded by another hundred) to participate in the RSD launch."

Kurtz began calling record stores outside of the coalitions to evangelize Record Store Day and to see if they would come on board.

"It wasn't easy. There was a lot of anger about how record stores were treated during the years that mass merchants were selling CDs cheaper than the stores could buy them directly [from distributors]. Some store owners assumed I was 'the man' when I called to ask if they would join us for this thing called Record Store Day. Often I couldn't finish more than a few sentences before the store owner would hang the phone up on me. People were pissed."

CHAPTER THREE

Do You Wanna Dance?

"It wasn't like we knew what we were doing.
We were just making it up as we went along."
—Michael Kurtz

[2007–2008: Record Store Day finds a receptive major label in Warner Bros., more than 300 indie stores set sales records on April 18, 2008, with just fifteen limited-edition titles.]

LOS ANGELES HAS A BAD rep for what Frank Zappa called plastic people. And then there are the congested highways where it can often take two hours to drive six miles. Regardless, it became apparent to Michael Kurtz that living in Los Angeles would allow him to connect with the LA-based record companies, and movers and shakers of the record industry.

> "I'm not sure why, but business people seem to be more open to discussing new ways of doing things in Los Angeles than in New York. And then there is a spiritual aspect to LA. This is where young bands like The Doors first discovered Transcendental Meditation in the 1960s at the same time that the Beatles were discovering TM in the UK."

Kurtz attributes being able to acclimate to his new environs and meet the steep challenge of establishing Record Store Day with a vinyl focus to reading the book *The Mind: Its Projections and Multiple*

Facets, by Yogi Bhajan, a master of Kundalini yoga. The book seemed to have been written for him. An excerpt from *The Mind* illuminates why Kurtz found an internal peace that made his RSD mission possible:

> "This Projection has an amazing capacity to take in large amounts of information and sensory impressions. It is active. It develops skills and abilities quickly. It is especially good at understanding the relationships between many parts of a complex system or environment. It cultivates understanding like a web in many directions, all of which connect to a central purpose or area."

Kurtz explains how the book's message helped him approach his Record Store Day strategy to win over indie retailers, record labels, artists, and their management:

> "Really what happens in the beginning [of RSD] is I discover this mystic guru. I bought his book, which teaches you how to meditate. That is what made it possible for me to go to these meetings and be positive, see the best in people, and be the best person I could. That all comes out of learning how to meditate."

Kurtz was going to need all the help he could get to muster support for Levin's vinyl idea, irking some record stores that would remind him they sold CDs. Kurtz explained to them that artists were excited about vinyl. To appease the retailers clamoring for exclusive CDs, a few notable titles emerged on Record Store Day. Rand Foster, owner of the Long Beach, CA-based store Fingerprints, distinctly remembers on Record Store Day in 2009 a Queen CD, but not vinyl, consisting of live radio sessions being available. What jogged his memory? Most of the people in line came for the CD, and the store ordered only about twenty copies.

Prior to Record Store Day, CIMS executive director Andrea Paschal also recalls record labels not being receptive to licensing albums for vinyl. "We'd go to NARM and walk in with a list of [CD] best sellers, and ask, 'Can you guys make these on vinyl?' I remember some of those initial meetings had them ask, 'Seriously?'"

Kurtz understood their skepticism over changing the way things were done. He recalls a Los Angeles meeting he had in 2006 during which an EMI executive Darren Stupak, now a Sony Music executive, floated a scenario of how independent retailers could radically change the way it did business. "I had breakfast with Darren at a Silver Lake place called the Bright Spot, and I remember him asking me, 'What if we came up with a different way to work with record stores and record labels and distributors that wasn't dependent on co-op advertising? What if we gave you some money to develop a product or something that's beyond just us booking ads?'"

Kurtz realizes now that Darren's questions made Record Store Day possible because it created a product—RSD as an event—that then drove the marketing, flipping the usual way of doing business. End result: Record Store Day advertises the culture of record stores, which then sell the exclusive releases not available anywhere else.

"I worked on the project for two or three years before it became entirely established that it was all about vinyl. There was no business to speak of for new vinyl prior to Record Store Day. You couldn't go to a label and say, 'Hey, let's make some vinyl records, or even buy vinyl. Or, hey, let's do a marketing program or campaign around vinyl, or let's devote a section in the store to new vinyl.' None of those things existed at the time so everybody from both major labels to indie labels would say, 'That makes no sense. What are you talking about?' For the indie labels, I think it was especially hard because vinyl is expensive to make so we had to prove to them that if they made vinyl records, then record stores and music fans would buy them, and they wouldn't be asked by the stores if they could return unsold copies."

RSD gets Warner's blessing

Unlike other major labels, Warner Bros Records never entirely stopped pressing new vinyl, due to its parent corporate culture. At the time, Tom "Grover" Biery spearheaded all things vinyl for Warner, and Kurtz visited him in his Burbank office. A radio personality in the 1980s, Biery was told by an Ohio station's management that he would be known on the air as "Grover." The moniker stuck even after he started working radio promotion for Warner in 1990, initially in Cleveland and then Chicago. Kurtz remembers Biery being immediately receptive to the concept of RSD.

> "I came out of that Noise in the Basement meeting with Eric's voice in my head going, 'Hey, let's try to get vinyl. So I meet with Grover and ask, 'Hey, can we do this thing called Record Store Day and press vinyl?' He says, 'I'm thinking of doing the same thing. This is perfect, let's marry the two of them together?' This is all in hindsight; it wasn't like we knew what we were doing. We were just spitballing. And then it just became a real thing."

Looking back on that meeting more than fourteen years later, Kurtz remembers wondering whether Grover might have been high because the label exec appeared a little too enthusiastic about his vision for Record Store Day. "I don't have any idea," says Grover, of whether he was under the influence that day. "I don't think that was the case to tell you the truth, and it would have been abnormal for me, but anything's possible." He adds an anecdote: "The last time I saw Kurtz, we had breakfast and he gave me an edible."

Warner getting behind Record Store Day made sense in 2007 because it "certainly fit in with the culture of Warner. It's been an artist-driven record company forever," Grover points out, offering some context to why he was so receptive to the RSD campaign.

"The community and the culture of record stores created who I am, to this day. My first real job was working in a record store at Jim's Records in Pittsburgh," Grover says, adding that its owner, Jim Spitznagel, helped him land his Warner job, even after working in radio. Grover never gave up being a record collector, remembering that while he worked the overnight shift as a DJ in the mid-1980s at a Youngstown radio station he drove ninety minutes to his favorite Pittsburgh record store to buy an import. "I still go to record stores constantly," notes Grover, who now operates his own label Slow Down Sounds, but in the fall of 2007, he ran a major record label.

> "I was running Warner Bros Records day to day at that point,
> I was general manager or EVP, so I had a lot of freedom.
> I just took [RSD] to heart. That's when we really dove deep
> into putting out really great sounding records on vinyl in
> 2006. At Warner, we always had artists who wanted vinyl.
> As a company, we were definitely predisposed to that idea.
> Back in the day with Mo Ostin and Lenny Waronker through
> Russ Thyret and Tom Whalley, the culture at Warner [vinyl]
> mattered to us. In general, we were a company that was
> open to those types of ideas. So Michael came in, maybe
> with Eric Levin and Don VanCleave, and they basically
> pitched the idea. I said, 'That sounds like an amazing idea.
> How much do you need?' It took very little time to think
> Record Store Day was a great idea and for us to champion it
> and still champion it."

Helping Grover champion Warner's involvement in RSD was longtime Warner Music Group consultant Jeff Bowers. "In the beginning, it was really just Jeff and I who kept driving [Record Store Day]," Kurtz explains, crediting Bowers as an unsung hero of why RSD became a success. "[Bowers] kept making sure shit would happen that was supposed to happen," Kurtz adds. "Jeff would just not take no for an answer. That's how it happened, really. Grover would tell Jeff, 'That's great' and Jeff would make it happen. Nothing would have happened without Bowers."

Prior to RSD, Warner was already working on Doors and Metallica boxed sets on vinyl, explains Bowers, who now runs a management company that has signed TikTok artists to major label deals. In 2007, Bowers had been a consultant to three Warner labels for about ten or eleven years, and the top executives, including Grover, Tom Whalley, and Craig Kallman, all wanted to do vinyl. "Within three months, every pressing plant and every mastering studio, every printer was full [with Warner work]," Bowers says.

To find vinyl capacity, Bowers contacted his Arizona childhood friend Eric Astor, whose company Furnace served as a vinyl broker for the large German pressing plant Pallas. Furnace opened its own pressing plant in 2018 in Alexandria, Virginia. Armed with the Warner order, Furnace also made a deal with Dutch pressing plant Record Industry, an operation previously owned by Sony. (Universal and Warner also pulled out of manufacturing vinyl for themselves years ago.)

Bowers, who was involved with Record Store Day from 2007 until 2014, remembers that Kurtz would visit Warner three times a week to push RSD, but he realized that they needed manufacturing help because audiophile and punk labels were still pressing records, along with a smattering of jazz and hip-hop. In advance of the first RSD, Bowers managed the production of various Warner Music Group exclusives, including a seven-inch Built to Spill single adorned by a cover by the band's leader Doug Martsch (who's also a comic book artist) and also a double single from R.E.M.

Regarding the three coalitions that banded together under the RSD banner, Bowers remarks, "Everyone loves those guys. Michael had the mindset that the indie stores are integral tastemakers." However, Bowers also remembers in RSD's early days encountering other industry people being skeptical with negative comments like "it's not going to work." "People were like, 'Why are you doing this?' Everyone loves vinyl now, but it wasn't always like that. We really had to push a rock up a hill. Everything about it was diametrically opposed to where the industry was," notes Bowers. But the naysayers were overlooking that vinyl was never completely over largely because of independent labels. Still, for vinyl to catch on again in a big way, increased pressing capacity was necessary. Bower adds:

> "Indie labels were getting mad at us because they couldn't get their records pressed. Michael came in and had this great idea for Record Store Day. We got crazy and realized we can really rejuvenate [vinyl]. Eric [Astor] then told Pallas and Record Industry, 'I can do 100,000 Metallica records if you give me a brokering deal,' so we did that. And then Michael came in, and said, 'Hey, let's do this together.' It made things fun again for artists."

FOR REASONS I'LL NEVER QUITE *understand, the rock department at Bristol Music Center was in the basement of the four-story store, but walking in there felt like the ultimate rush. I never knew what was going to await me. I never knew what newfound gem was going to be blaring out of the speakers. All I knew was that something incredible would happen because it always did. It was all about the possibilities and the possibilities were infinite. Like a kid in a candy store, except my version of that was…a kid in a record store.*

From the mid-1970s to the early 1980s, the rock department at Bristol Music Center in Copenhagen, Denmark, was the most significant part of my life outside school and family, and probably often tied right in there with both. My dad had started taking me there as early as I could remember, and the early excursions felt like going to another world. Growing up, I thought my dad was the coolest guy, and no place was more "next level" than his music room in our pad, which housed one of the vastest record collections around town in the sixties. Going up to that hang space on the top floor was actually like going to a record store. There were thousands of records, scattered all over—in the racks, on the furniture, on the shelves, next to the record player. Charlie Parker, Miles Davis, John Coltrane, the Doors, the Rolling Stones, Janis Joplin…the list is endless. And after my dad dragged me to see Deep Purple in 1973, I acquired the Fireball *album the next day, and began attempting to amass a collection worthy of my father's.*

Ken and Ole, who were the guys responsible for the rock department at Bristol, were my heroes. Whatever they recommended instantly became a must-have. In 1979, when I got invited back to Ken's apartment to check out his personal record collection, it was one of the most exciting things in my life. Period. After I moved to the United States in the early eighties, they became my lifeline to European hard rock, and the packages they would send me on a monthly basis were the most invigorating, life-affirming element.

As that showed up in my mailbox, I would sit for hours with my records; listening, looking, imagining, transporting myself to some other dimension, as the music enveloped me and carried me as far away as my imagination could take me. And the covers! Those record sleeves kept me fixated on the bands, musicians, lyrics, and imagery being thrown in my direction. I kept logs over what records I would listen to and how many times I would listen to them. In other words, I was obsessed. I lived and breathed in a record universe, day in, day out.

Boy, do I miss those days!

As times have changed, records unfortunately play a significantly different role in most young people's lives and have primarily become a niche entity. But there are signs of hope. My seventeen-year-old asked for a record player for his birthday two years ago, and I have been steadily doing my best due diligence as a parent, feeding him the classics since then. This process reached its emotional peak (and I even got misty-eyed!) when he put Deep Purple's Machine Head and Made in Japan on his latest Christmas wish list, in good old vinyl format. What a moment! Maybe it all will work out after all...

As music becomes available either through only the internet or in gigantic airport-size retail stores, it is more important than ever—actually vital—that all us fanatics continue to bring to light the importance of records, and to support to the maximum of our abilities the independent record store outlet. The good news is, of course, that vinyl is making a measurable comeback. But that is not enough for us to rest on our laurels. We must all bond continuously together and scream from every rooftop with our loudest voices, enlighten our kids, fly the flag, and beat the drum (!) to the best of our ability.

For music.

For vinyl.

For independent record stores.

For people like you and me who live and breathe music twenty-four hours a day.

By the way, I'm still wondering why the rock department was in the basement of the Bristol Music Center. Of course, the cynical side of me wonders if it has anything to do with the fact that rock somehow is perceived by self-appointed musical purists as a lesser form of music? Don't even get me started on that one! Right now, let's focus on having a Record Store with a basement to whine about in the first place and maybe we will finish that conversation some other day...

—Lars Ulrich of Metallica,
2016 Record Store Day Ambassador

CHAPTER FOUR

Enter Metallica

"Rasputin was the biggest store that could handle 600 Metallica fans...."

[2008: This popular metal band signs autographs and poses for photos with fans for six hours in Northern California on the first RSD.]

HAVING A MAJOR ARTIST SUPPORT record stores was critical for Record Store Day to succeed in Michael Kurtz's mind. At the top of his list was Metallica, one of the highest grossing touring and biggest selling bands of the twenty-first century. "My understanding is that James Hetfield and Lars Ulrich formed the band, but it's Lars who kind of leads the band," says Kurtz, of the band's drummer/ spokesman who "worked in a record store and always made really cool stuff for fans." With the help of Don VanCleave, Kurtz began working with Metallica's day-to-day manager, Marc Reiter of Q Prime, to see if the band would be a part of the Record Store Day event by doing an in-store at their hometown record store, Rasputin Music, an independent chain of record stores first opened in 1971 by Ken Sarachan. His goal was to own a record store big enough to offer every album made.

As it turned out, Lars needed no convincing for Metallica to be involved in RSD as they were working with Warner Bros. on the possible reissue of Metallica albums on vinyl. If it worked, Metallica would do an event for fans at the record store and release albums on vinyl. When asked, the entire band was in favor of meeting their fans at Rasputin and to help Record Store Day get off the ground with the vinyl reissues.

Was Kurtz concerned at all that Ulrich was portrayed negatively seven years earlier for suing Napster? "Not at all. I totally dug Lars for having the clarity of mind and the guts to stand up to a journalist like PBS's Charlie Rose and essentially say something to the effect of 'Napster never asked us if we wanted to go along with what they were doing and it's totally uncool,'" says Kurtz, who believed the internet platform that Napster created wasn't all that revolutionary or innovative. "I remember a lot of people had similar ideas at the time for what would become streaming and YouTube, but didn't think it was okay to pirate the music and videos that artists made. We wanted bands to be successful and be paid for what they do, not steal their livelihood.

To make Record Store Day an extraordinary event, it was agreed that on April 19, 2008, Metallica would meet fans at Rasputin Music in Mountain View, California, coinciding with the reissue on vinyl of the band's first two albums, *Kill 'Em All* and *Ride the Lightning*. "Rasputin was big enough to handle up to eight hundred Metallica fans comfortably," explains Kurtz, but it would require secrecy and the ability to orchestrate a major in-store artist event. So he brought into the plan Steve Duncan, then Rasputin's district manager and head buyer, a few months before any of his coworkers. Rasputin had hosted hundreds and hundreds of bands, but this one required special attention.

"Michael Kurtz gave me a call probably two months prior and kind of hinted that it was a possibility," remembers Duncan, adding that he soon also heard from a member of Metallica's management team. "Everyone [at Rasputin] was elated," he adds, admitting that because RSD was in its early stages, "I'm not sure ninety-nine percent of the people knew what it was. We were working toward this day. And no one knew what it was going to be."

Metallica diehards, of course, showed up in droves. "We had people in line three days prior to the event. People from Australia, the UK, South Africa, from all over." Duncan remembers that the first one hundred fans were handpicked by the band's fan club, and that morning Rasputin staff handed out as many as eight hundred wristbands. Meanwhile, the store—located in the same space occupied by a former Tower Records—opened that morning to the throng of ecstatic fans. Metallica provided—free of charge—commemorative posters and T-shirts for the fans. "They were signing guitars, they were signing posters. They made sure that everybody in that line was really taken care of. It was really pretty cool," Duncan remembers. The only extra cost to Rasputin was tripling the store staff that day to handle the crowds and increased activity at the registers, even though they were only letting in groups of between ten and fifteen people at a time "just to keep it manageable and keep it safe."

Across the country all of the hard work evangelizing record stores and vinyl paid off with Record Store Day events by Built to Spill, The Black Angels, Regina Spektor, Nada Surf, the Black Rebel Motorcycle Club, Rogue Wave, Kate Nash, and Janelle Monae, among others. The day after, the word spread like wildfire from store to store that something extraordinary had just occurred. Record stores had done it; Record Store Day was a massive success. But how?

CHAPTER FIVE

Message to Love

"Folks who work here are professors. Don't replace all the knowers with guessors keep'em open. They're the ears of the town."
—Tom Waits

[Musicians send en masse how they found their livelihoods hanging out in record stores.]

FOR MOST TEENAGE MUSICIANS, THEIR local record stores seemed like school. It's where they met future bandmates, talked about their love of music, some even worked the cash registers years ago with the hope their music would be purchased there one day. Beginning early 2008, the testimonials started pouring in from musicians and other record store-loving celebrities.

Paul McCartney: There's nothing as glamorous to me as a record store. When I recently played Amoeba in LA, I realized what fantastic memories such a collection of music brings back when you see it all in one place. This is why I'm more than happy to support Record Store Day, and I hope that these kinds of stores will be there for us all for many years to come.

Chris Frantz (Talking Heads and Tom Tom Club): To me, indie record stores are a place to make new discoveries or to find music that you knew about but thought was lost. Most of these stores know their best customers by name and will happily make a recommendation of what's new, cool, and amazing. These are the places where surprising new bands are featured alongside the all-time greats. Record stores are also great places to hang out and gossip about whatever's going on, musically or otherwise. They are the safe haven for the music nerd who can't get enough inside information about the bands and artists he loves. My own personal favorite is La La Land in The Hague. I'm still mourning the loss of Secret Sounds in Fairfield, Connecticut, but at least I've got the T-shirt.

Booker T. (Booker T. & the MG's): They were a library and a breeding ground for me when I was growing up—that's where I got all my influences and how I learned to play. I was reminded of that yesterday at Criminal Records.

Brett Gurewitz (Bad Religion and founder of Epitaph Records): I got my start by going around to record stores like Moby Disc and Middle Earth and giving them "The Bad Religion" seven-inch to sell on consignment. I'd go back every couple of weeks to see if they needed any more, and while I was at it I'd always check out the zines, flyers, and new punk releases. These places were more than stores, they were gathering places and hubs of information. They were the heart of the LA hardcore scene, and it would never have existed without them.

Neko Case: I love the smell of them. I love that people actually care for and know about the music they are selling.

Jeff Tweedy (Wilco): My introduction to all this great music and to "the music business" came from hanging around and eventually working at independent record stores. Nothing beats browsing in your favorite store, listening to music, finding something new or old that you've been searching for, all that. And without these stores, there's just no way Wilco would still be around.

Colin Meloy (The Decemberists): I don't know what I would do without indie record stores. Having grown up in a town without them, I can tell you that it's no fun to shop for indie records at chain box stores. Independent record stores like Sonic Boom in Seattle, Rockin Rudys in Missoula, and 2nd Avenue in Portland were holy golden shrines to me growing up. Actually, they still are.

Adam Duritz (Counting Crows): I feel like I spent most of my life wandering the aisles of record stores. I used to love going to Amoeba when our guitar player Immy (David Immerglück) worked there and hanging out all day talking about records. I think that's what finally got him fired; there were always people trailing around after him cluttering up the store trying to soak up the "Immerwisdom." Actually, now that I think about it, I'm pretty sure it was when some kid came up to the cash register with a pile of records, and Immy, who was sitting on top of the counter at the time, grabbed the pile, perused it, threw most of them to the side, and said something like, "Forget these, you don't need them. These two are really good, that one is great. Now go to that rack over there and grab the new Gang of Four and the Pere Ubu album. That's all you need." It probably would've been cool if the manager hadn't walked up behind him just before he did it. Oh well.

Mike Scully (The Simpsons writer): One of my most vivid record store memories was being in Belmont Records in Springfield, Massachusetts, when the first shipment of Bruce Springsteen's *Darkness on the Edge of Town* arrived. I helped the manager, John Dougan, unpack the boxes. We pulled out the first two copies, looked at the great cover shot, then flipped it over to the list of songs on the back, imagining their greatness solely by their titles: "Badlands," "Candy's Room," "Racing In The Streets," "Prove It All Night," "Promised Land." How could they not be great songs with titles like these?! We put the album on the store's turntable, blasted it, and we were right—it was incredible. I must confess that I use iTunes and buy CDs online when I'm not near a record store, but I'll never have a moment like that sitting at my computer. I can't imagine what my life would have been without all the hours and money I "wasted" in record stores. (My father's word, not mine.)

Robyn Hitchcock: Records used to mean vinyl, then cassettes, then CDs, and now downloads. Like currency, they got smaller and are now almost invisible. The record stores were a great network where music fans could listen to what was out there without necessarily having to buy it. But if they did, they came away with a black disc (unless it was pink or green or red or purple or a photograph), embedded with grooves, mostly enshrined in a cardboard sleeve that contained vital additions to the music inside. These sacred objects (and their slightly less sacred descendants, the tape and the compact disc) were the closest you could get to the act itself: like portable shrines with holy relics. Scott McCaughey, Peter Buck, and Bill Rieflin, who comprise the Venus 3, my American band, all heard my songs for the first time in the record stores where they worked. It's probable they also first heard each other's music like that, too. I have fond memories of hanging out in US record shops, particularly the Used Record Shoppe in the Sunset district of San Francisco. Shops like Let It Be in Minneapolis, Bill's in Dallas, Tower on Fourth and Broadway (NYC), Easy Street in Seattle, Criminal in Atlanta, Amoeba in LA, and many others gave us a platform to perform live on tour and unfailingly stocked our records (Robyn Hitchcock & the Egyptians, my solo work, The Soft Boys, and, now, me & the Venus 3) where the larger chains found us unprofitable. Independent record stores gave my career a solid base: people who got into your stuff that way really got into it. Now technology and economics are leading away from physical product, and from the sale of records in record stores. Hopefully some will survive as boutique oases where music lovers can browse and meet not just the music but each other. You can't get everything through the post…

Lil Boosie: When no one else was supporting me…the mom and pops (record stores) would sell my music. I had been out here for ten years and before the [record] deal....It was the mom and pops that were feeding my family.

John Mellencamp: Immersing yourself in the environment of a real record store where music is celebrated and cherished adds real value to the experience of buying music. In some ways, that retail experience is as important as the music.

Bruce Springsteen: I buy CDs all the time. I'll go into a record store and just buy $500 worth of CDs. I will! I am single-handedly supporting what's left of the record business. I hate to see record stores disappear, and I'm old-school in that I think you should pay for your music. But what my kids do is download a lot of things, pay for them, and then if they love something, they'll get the CD. That may be the future.

Ben Harper: Independent record stores are much more than the name suggests. They are an international community and platform where music has an outlet and an opportunity to grow over the long term, in a way that sincerely connects with community and culture. They are also a magnificent mob of highly opinionated musical bandits, which I am proud to call my pals! Bill, keep that Indian ring shining for me. Matt, I'll meet you in the morning for breakfast. John, we'll always have Paris. Rhino...straight outta Claremont!

Exene Cervenka (X): The reason I am touring independent record stores from San Diego to Seattle this April is that I want to play for free, to people of all ages, at a reasonable hour, in a place we love to be. I'm touring at my own expense, because I don't want the economy to stand between my music and people that might want to hear it. Bring your X records, the kids, shop independent, and let's have a party!

Joe Satriani: Independent record stores are a vital source of the ever-changing cool. They respond to the street faster than the chains can. They help us telegraph to each other what's "now" and what's not, what we should be telling our friends and neighbors about, and what's about to take off, or no longer hot. Musical trends are confirmed at the local independent record store, by you and me. Hanging out, listening to something you've never heard before, being enlightened by the staff, getting into something new, finding that old recording you've been searching for, having your local band's newest offering stocked right next to major label stuff, it all happens at the local indie shop. Why would we want to do away with all that?"

Nellie McKay: Independent record stores are aural cathedrals, havens for those who find music as much a spiritual endeavor as passing entertainment. Indie employees will go out of their way to help you find a rare or back-catalogued recording, commiserating over neglected artists and all-but-forgotten masterpieces. They offer discounts and suggest records they enjoy with genuine interest and enthusiasm. Indies embody mom and pop, individualist expression—they're in it for love, not to turn a huge profit or to bend popular taste to a uniform will. Viva la indie.

Pat Monahan (Train): Independent record stores have been a major part of my life as a musician, as well as a fan of music. Raspberries in Erie, Pennsylvania, was my first visit. It was a wonderland of my potential future. Stores from Birmingham to San Francisco have been turning people into lifelong fans of my music, Train's and countless other bands and artists for as long as I can remember. I miss being able to see a great Independent music store as often as I used to. With that said though, they are still as strong a contributor to the music business as ever. They're where I got my start. Thank you all!

Joe Principe (Rise Against): I think record stores play a huge part in discovering new music. When I was growing up, I would spend hours going through all the bins looking for something new that seemed interesting to me and that could relate to what I was listening to at the time. This is why I want to support National Record Store Day.

Andrew WK: One of the most amazing places in the world is a record store called either Liberty Street Recordings or Encore Records. It's located in the great town of Ann Arbor, Michigan. Many of my friends worked there, and I spent a lot of time there during high school. One time I went in, and this woman who I think owned the place was listening to Black Sabbath's *Sabbath Bloody Sabbath* very loudly. She was probably the same age as my mom and looked like a librarian. After the album side finished, she said, "God, I just love what that man's voice does to me."

Klaus Meine (Scorpions): It was in a tiny little record store back in the early 1960s in my hometown of Hannover, West Germany, where I would put the headphones on to listen to a rare song that was really hard to find in those days. "My Bonnie" by Tony Sheridan & the Beat Brothers (later known as The Beatles) rocked my heart and started a passion that never left me…RECORD STORE DAY FOREVER.

Matthew Caws (Nada Surf): My first job was in a basement record store on Cornelia Street, just off the corner of Sixth Avenue and West Fourth Street in Manhattan. It was called Record Runner at the time. I was seventeen years old. I'd made friends with the owner, and when he went on tour with his band, he asked me to cover for him. I worked by myself. The store was being sold to a new owner soon, so no new stock was coming in. We didn't take credit cards. There were stacks of old British rock magazines. All I did was sell, listen, read, and snack. It's still the best job I ever had. When Nada Surf got dropped after our first album and I couldn't pay the rent anymore, I worked at Earwax in Williamsburg. Part of the charm of that store was how idiosyncratically it was stocked. The store's contents reflected the taste of the owners and the people working there long enough to put in orders. Plenty of Vietnamese psych rock but no Elvis Costello. I think they have some now, but I'm sure there's something else "standard" they don't have. On Sundays, I worked with Alex Holden, who ended up drawing the cover of [Nada Surf's fourth album] *The Weight Is a Gift.* [Working at Earwax] is still the other best job I've ever had. Unless there's somewhere I have to be in a hurry, I go into every record store I see. When one closes, I mourn the loss. I have made great acquaintances and a few lifelong friends at record stores. Music has given me more wonder, solace, and excitement than anything else in life. It is great that it's so easy to get music online, but there is nothing like flipping through stacks of the real thing. With SO MUCH music out there, having a real person curate a real store is completely invaluable and irreplaceable. Please go visit at least one store on Record Store Day and buy at least one record or CD. You'll be doing your part to conserve a priceless institution.

Dave Schools (Widespread Panic): When I was a kid, the indie record store was the basket house of my generation. It was a hub where I could go to hang out and hear music that the radio sure as hell was never going to play. I was exposed to new artists, and I met like-minded listeners. Sometimes an artist would actually come into the store and perform or "meet the people," and to me that was the epitome of cool. Without the inspiration I was exposed to by my local record store, I would never have been able to make the music that has made me a happier person. It is important that we support the remaining independent stores so that we can preserve the whole food chain that stretches from the artists' hands to the listener's ears. So skip the big-box retailers and their price-point indices. Vote for the little guy, and while you're at it, why not ask your local indy record store when they are going to start serving coffee?

Peter Gabriel: I was introduced to lots of great music through my local record store. It was a place where people knew music and they knew me and could make great suggestions and discoveries. Whether it is in the physical world or online, the value of a great and knowledgeable record store has not gone away.

David and Don Was (Was Not Was): In the beginning was the record store, more like a modern-day temple with its attendant priesthood and initiates, a holy repository of the culture's most sacred beats and rhymes. By comparison, the internet is a clean room in a hospital—it lacks the funk and feeling of a place with floors and ceilings and racks full of soul-stirring goodness. May they persist until someone turns the lights out on this small planet! Here's to the true believers. Keep the faith, brothers, and sisters!

Amanda Palmer (Dresden Dolls): My early record shopping experiences were my musical backdrop. It's not just the ability to touch, see, and smell an album and the artwork…it's the fact that you are in a real place with real people…and not just any people: other music-obsessed freaks like you. I discovered so many bands by just hanging out, talking to shopkeepers, getting recommendations from some random dude who was flipping through the Nick Cave bootleg box as fervently as I was. Every time I am in a different city on tour, I make a point to hit the indie retail record stores to see what they're spinning and selling, because I just LOVE being there…my own personal and sometimes anonymous church. You can't get that feeling sitting behind your computer, ever.

Shelby Lynne: You can't roll a joint on an iPod. Buy vinyl!

Brett Netson (Built To Spill): The local record store is a cultural event. Every purchase you make, every day, every year, it is a rich cultural history in the making. Go down to your favorite shop and grab some coffee, a nice pastry, and then head into the record store for the ultimate recorded experience. Maybe see some friends. Next thing you know you just had a nice afternoon. Go to one of those big-box stores and get the full assault. Bright sterile fluorescent lights and all that fake, old timey crap on the walls that drives home the point that this is an approximation of an experience. You are one of a million cattle herded in and out of those crapholes. This history can easily be rewritten. And you sure as hell won't talk to anyone there, cause everyone else is just as annoyed, alienated, and lost as you are. And, as you get trapped in that endless parking lot, it really seals the deal. I have precious memories of my favorite shops and so do many of my best friends. That's a shared history, man. And buying my first Velvet Underground record or Love's *Forever Changes*, or seeing my first "punk show" flyer, takes that whole experience deep into you. That lasts forever. That's powerful stuff.

Mike Patton (Faith No More): I love indie record stores! My first job was working at a record store. While touring, I still always hit my favorite record stores. What is not to love about record stores? To be surrounded by millions of records, some that you know and love and others that are hidden treasures waiting to be discovered. Record stores are also a great social outing. You can meet and talk to other people that share your love for the art of music. The excitement of strolling the aisles of a cool record store will always excite me. It's best to do it without knowing what you are looking for. I can spend hours in my favorite record store. Record stores are my candy shops!

Cameron Crowe (director of *Almost Famous*): The record store. Where true fandom begins. It's the soul of discovery, and the place where you can always return for that mighty buzz. The posters. The imports. The magazines. The discerning clerks, paid in vinyl, professors of the groove. Long live that first step inside, when the music envelopes you and you can't help it. You walk up to the counter and ask the question that begins the journey, "What are you playing?" Long live the record store and the guys and girls who turn the key, and unlock those dreams, every day.

John Doe (X): The physical act of picking up a recording (CD, vinyl, cassette), checking it out, finding something unavailable, etc., is an experience you will NEVER get online. And now it's becoming common knowledge that CDs have more digital information than most files, so they sound better. A great or even good record store is like no other.

Damon Albarn (Blur and Gorilllaz): My local independent record shop (Honest Jons) is a library where you can go to listen to music, learn about it, exchange ideas about it, and be inspired by it. I think independent record shops will outlive the music industry as we know it because long term their value to people is far greater, because even in our era of file-sharing and blogs, you can't replace the actual look on someone's face when they are playing something they really rate and think you should listen to it too. It's special.

Noel Gallagher (Oasis): Record shops were really important when I was growing up. It's something that's in my DNA. I think if we can keep record shops open for as long as possible, we owe it to the young people of this country. For this year's Record Store Day, I'll be getting involved. I've got something unique coming out. Hopefully the fans will like it, and they'll keep the flame burning for your local record shop.

Joan Jett: The indie record stores are the backbone of recorded music culture. It's where we go to network, browse around, and find new songs to love. The stores whose owners and staff live for music have spread the word about exciting new things faster and with more essence than either radio or the press. Any artist that doesn't support the wonderful ma and pa record stores across America is contributing to our own extinction.

Ziggy Marley: Record stores keep human social contact alive; it brings people together. Without the independent record stores the community breaks down with everyone sitting in front of their computers.

Wayne Coyne (The Flaming Lips): The cool record store. It is where you can talk to people who are like you. They look like you, think like you, and, most tellingly, like the same music as you. The only comparable experience these days would probably be an art museum, an actual place where you can stand and simply be surrounded by your heroes. Music is an important part of our culture and record stores play a vital part in keeping the power of music alive.

Henry Rollins: I have watched independent record stores evaporate all over America and Europe. That's why I go into as many as I can and buy records whenever possible. If we lose the independent record store, we lose big.

Robert Trujillo (Metallica): Record Store Day for me has opened so many doors, and Michael Kurtz has just been an angel for me on so many levels, whether it's through Metallica or *Jaco* (the official Record Store Day film about the iconic bass player). He'll always be there for me. We're kind of two individuals that we just get really inspired by challenges and trying different things. When the opportunities are there, it's always nice to kind of get his input and opinion and collaborate when we can. Record Store Day is a great platform for all types of music. It can be punk, funk, jazz, classical, country, and they celebrate the rare stuff. They love the rawness, the purity. That's great because you're celebrating that organic matter of a composition [in a home studio] because it's nice to hear the preliminary existence of a piece. Recording at some high-end studio, which is great too. Michael Kurtz is totally into that too.

Chuck Berry: Music is an important part of our culture and record stores play a vital part in keeping the power of music alive.

Elton John: I love record stores. When I became famous, I used to help out [at a London shop] on Saturdays when one of the guys wanted to go for lunch. I'd help behind the counter because I loved to see what people chose. I can go to the record store in Vegas and spend three hours, just the smell of it and the memories. Music has been my whole life. It's been my crutch. It's been my soul mate. [In Los Angeles] I used to go at nine o'clock on Tuesday mornings before anyone was in Tower Records to see the new releases. I cried when Tower Records left the strip. But I'm glad that record shops and small record shops are beginning to pop up with vinyl everywhere I go. I sold my original vinyl collection in 1990 to raise money for the Elton John Foundation. It was the first thing I did for the foundation. I sold the whole collection, singles and everything, for about $250,000. I hated getting rid of it. I started collecting CDs, but it wasn't the same. Two years ago, I found a store in Las Vegas called Wax Trax Records. I can spend three hours there. I started collecting vinyl slowly and replacing what I'd sold. Kind of long story short now, I have seven thousand pieces of vinyl. I buy most of my new records from Rough Trade in London. They know me and send me a list every week to find out what I want. And I buy five or six new albums a week on vinyl. It's just something about the tactile nature of it. I love the ritual of it, just the wonder and process of putting the needle down and the sound coming out. It does sound better, but I know people say, "No, it doesn't." I've been in so many studios. I've made so many records. It certainly does sound better. I look at the sleeve, especially the old albums with the liner note. Record Store Day is just a great example to celebrate vinyl.

CHAPTER SIX
Money Changes Everything

*"Best day ever, and then the next year would be
the best day ever, and so on...."*

*[2008–2009: With the concept proven, Record Store Day ratchets up its
overall potential with eighty-five limited edition titles planned for the
next year as more record labels jump on the bandwagon.]*

THE FIRST RECORD STORE DAY exceeded everyone's moderate
expectations. All of the objectives were met: 1) create excitement for
the three hundred participating US record stores and bring attention
to the importance they play in their communities; 2) pretty much
sell out the seventeen exclusive titles; 3) disprove the theory that no
one is interested in physical media in the age of iTunes; 4) prove
to independent and major record labels that selling limited editions
could be a viable business model; and 5) demonstrate with actual
sales numbers that vinyl is not dead.

Andrea Paschal, who started working at CIMS in 2005 and
now heads the coalition, recalls the phone calls she received from
her organization's members during the first Record Store Day:
"Best day ever, and then the next year that would be the best day
ever, and so on."

Her CIMS boss Don VanCleave sums up what was accomplished
on April 19, 2008:

"So we got the records all out there and then kind of held our breath on the day of the first Record Store Day. I started getting calls late in the afternoon from some [CIMS] stores. We weren't quite texting yet, our age group anyway. I started getting notes and messages from store owners that it was their 'biggest day ever, lines at the door, first chance I've had to communicate, we're swamped, Oh, my God, can we do this again next week'. Everybody had record days, record Aprils, record everything. It was pretty awesome."

"One of the reasons why I think that Record Store Day was able to blow up the way it did so quickly, was because everybody was being asked to do the things that they already know how to do," reflects Maine-based Bull Moose's Chris Brown. "Stores had bands in-store [appearances and performances]. We put stuff on sale. Record companies put out records. So it wasn't like anybody had to come up with a new process. Everybody already knows what [stores] are great at…[RSD prompted them] to do it at the same time."

Meanwhile, on the West Coast—and virtually everywhere in between—the Long Beach, California, record store Fingerprints also experienced an awesome first Record Store Day that fell into place exactly according to plan. "Out of the gate, we had a pretty damn strong Record Store Day," reflects Fingerprints owner Rand Foster. Performing talent at the store include popular band the Silversun Pickups, and Judas Priest's Rob Halford did a signing for his project Fight.

Labels saw an opportunity to provide promotional swag, such as free stickers and CD samplers promoting their bands' latest releases. Across the country, all of the hard work evangelizing record stores and vinyl paid off with Record Store Day events by Built To Spill, The Black Angels, Regina Spektor, Nada Surf, Black Rebel Motorcycle Club, Rogue Wave, Kate Nash, and Janelle Monae, among others. The day after, the word spread like wildfire from store to store that something extraordinary had just occurred. Record stores had done it; Record Store Day was a massive success.

But how? All the stores would reconvene for another Noise In The Basement (NITB) in Baltimore in September 2008 where they could trade notes on what went right and bask in their collective success. Kurtz planned the second NITB to be a massive party that no record store would want to miss.

> "Fun was at the center of what we would do with Record Store Day going forward. The artists who met, performed, and hung with us at that second Noise In The Basement were pretty amazing: Hold Steady, Rage Against The Machine's Tom Morello, Noah & the Whale, Serena Ryder, Nappy Roots, Motörhead, The Pretenders, and Janelle Monae. We also had fun crossing over into other media by inviting cast members of HBO's *The Wire* to talk with us. We were even a part of the filming of the Food Network's Baltimore-based show *Ace of Cakes*. In the episode, an awesome cake was baked, and we appeared in a softball game that pitted record store owners (all wearing Metal Blade T-shirts) against record labels. This idea of having fun, and throwing a party for record stores, got baked into the Record Store Day discussion to come."

Farewell Junketboy, Hello ThinkIndie

But Don VanCleave dropped something of a bombshell at the second Noise in the Basement by announcing his resignation from CIMS and Junketboy after twenty years in indie retail. He was going into management for Gary Gersh's Artists Organization.

Michael Bunnell, VanCleave's successor at CIMS and JunketBoy, remembers being astounded by the news.

> "The entire CIMS organization was quite surprised. Don had been with us since the start of the organization in 1995. We had started with a group of tough independent music store

owners who never thought they belonged to any organized music group because they were too independent. What we ended up with by 2008 was an organized group of stores who not only formed an alliance to do collective marketing, but opened a distribution company, and also filled a role as a voice in the industry for the independent music store sector. It was a big deal [for VanCleave] to walk away from but I think Don had his sights on other career possibilities."

Bunnell, who had an insider view of RSD's tremendous growth both from the CIMS vantage point as well as store owner (The Record Exchange in Boise, Idaho), wasn't planning on being VanCleave's heir apparent.

"I had been on the CIMS board since the second year it was formed, helped write the organizational documents, and been the CIMS board chair for a few years by then. I guess I saw it as an opportunity to further my career, but really I simply saw it as a chance to help a group of people and stores I really cared about. When he left his [CIMS] role we knew we needed to change the name from JunketBoy [to ThinkIndie]. By the time I took over in his role, a lot of those industry perks (e.g., all-expense paid trips; backstage passes at Wembley) were history, dammit. Don had a great talent as a showman, me not so much."

Meanwhile, the record companies realized Record Store Day wasn't some flash in the pan, and it behooved them to jump onto the Record Store Day bandwagon. The sales numbers proved consumers wanted new vinyl. Not surprisingly, in April 2009 the second list of exclusive RSD products would expand exponentially to *eighty-five* titles. Kurtz says that a logistical headache did not emerge from the expanded list.

"At this point, it was all opportunities. We quickly set up distribution of the RSD promotional items with ThinkIndie, and they handled that. If there were any headaches at this point, it was coming mainly from record store owners who were skeptical of the concept. They thought it was being run by the majors but it wasn't. I was the guy who made the rounds trying to get everyone to understand what we were doing."

Bunnell puts RSD's tremendous growth into perspective:

"By the second year, we knew we had something that had a huge potential to change the way the industry and the world saw the independent music store. We had lost literally thousands of stores across the country and the world. Our clientele was aging, and we were losing youthful consumers in the stores. With Record Store Day being a major contributor to the rebirth of vinyl, it helped save the stores and get an entire generation interested in a format that we had always loved. Young people turned from using music as background noise to focusing on it as the important art form it is. I know that sounds grand and overblown but it's the truth. It really focused people's appreciation of the physical product side of the music business. Music fans of all ages returned to the stores."

Unlike the full support from Warner, Sony was easing into vinyl, while Universal seemed skeptical whether vinyl was anything more than a fad at best. "They thought it was nice that we were doing Record Store Day, and even made a free sampler vinyl LP for the stores," Kurtz remembers. "But at that time they didn't see vinyl as more than a fad."

Meanwhile, Kurtz was still building support among a sometimes still skeptical group of independent record store owners. Amoeba Records' head buyer Brad Schelden, who in 2001 helped open the company's iconic Hollywood, California, store on Sunset Boulevard after working at its San Francisco store at Haight Ashbury, admits he wasn't so sure whether

RSD wasn't a flash in the pan, and the early success took him by surprise. "Honestly, we kind of thought it was silly: 'Record Store Day'? What is that? Since Amoeba had been doing its own thing for so long, the thinking around the company was, 'we don't need this' or 'we don't know what it's going to be about.' We didn't know what to expect from the customers either. 'Are they going to show up or are they going to care?' But I think right away that first year, we were like, 'Okay, this is the thing.'"

In the background, Kurtz soldiered on, googling record store names by city and state and making blind cold calls. It didn't always go well. "The owner of Rolling Stone Records in Chicago, hung up in a huff, for example, when I tried to explain it to him. At this point, most music that was sold to record stores by the labels/distributors was still on CD, so there was a very real push back from store owners about not creating CDs instead of vinyl for RSD, as well as the perceived favoritism towards the coalition stores."

Meanwhile, CIMS' contribution to Record Store Day's continued by distributing RSD releases and other exclusive products through ThinkIndie to the entire independent music store sector, according to Bunnell.

> "We never saw it as only for CIMS stores, unfortunately many record stores thought that was the case or that we were giving special consideration to our stores, that was never the case. All independent stores were and are treated exactly the same. We started the company as a result of the box stores producing original products for their stores only. We felt that was a bad industry move and pleaded with the labels and distributors that everyone should have equal access to all core products. They ignored our pleas so we just thought that we could play the same game, if forced, and produce and distribute products for the independent sector alone. That concept really led to Record Store Day taking the same posture and enabling products for the true believers, the independent record store."

A PERSON SHOULD HAVE A *personality. You won't get one dicking around on a computer. It helps to go somewhere where there are other people who are interested in something you are. That's how a record store or any shop that's got some life to it should work. It's not about selling shit. I got my name, my musical education, and my personality all from working at a record store during my tender years. Small indie shops have always been a mix of theater and laboratory. In the 1950s and 1960s, the teen kids used to gather after school at these places to listen free to the latest singles and see if they liked the beat. You could buy the disc you liked for seventy-nine cents and, if you were lucky, meet a chick. Clerks in these places became managers (like Brian Epstein), label heads (Jac Holzman) and faces on album covers (like me). Personally, I feel best in a store that, while staying small and socially relaxed, still keeps a complete variety of music types and nonmusical recordings on offer. I'm aware though that a lot of great places are genre-specific, like dancehall shops in Jamaica or specializing in compass here in [Miami's] Little Haiti. In Europe and on the West Coast the same goes on for punk and goth. All of this is cool and has a much bigger future than most people realize today. When the record and record store businesses began to die at the turn of the new century, they deserved it because they got too big, too boring, and too plastic.*

As Record Store Day Ambassador for 2012, I feel like a representative from some exotic jungle full of life and death and sex and anger, called upon to wear a leopard skin and translate joy to the world of the dead.

—Iggy Pop, 2012 Record Store Day Ambassador

CHAPTER SEVEN
Wild World

"It was an obviously great idea that started in America, and it just spread to the UK and other countries. It was kind of a no-brainer. The template had been drawn up."
—Martin Mills, Beggars Group

[2009–2011: On-site Coachella RSD store fuels early RSD growth; Canadian and British record shops follow US stores celebrating what they do, followed by Dutch, French, and German, and later throughout Europe, Asia, Africa, and South America.]

AMONG THE PARTIES THAT TOOK notice of Record Store Day's first-year success in getting people interested in buying vinyl again was the promoters of the huge Coachella Valley Music and Arts Festival, the annual music and arts festival near Palm Springs, California, held since 1999 at the same time of the year as RSD, always featuring the most popular and emerging musical artists. Coachella typically sets new records for festival attendance and gross revenues, drawing upward of a quarter million people.

Festival director Bill Fold contacted Michael Kurtz for a meeting to gauge interest in establishing an RSD store on the Coachella grounds. Kurtz was intrigued, initially not realizing the impact Record Store Day made in its first year but then recognizing the synergy between the two entities.

"I was shocked to hear him say something to the effect of, 'We've looked at the impact of Record Store Day and it's equal to or surpasses that of Coachella.' I was a bit stunned as I hadn't considered the size of what we'd done in that first year," Kurtz admits.

Consider the logistics of building a record store in the desert: temperatures can get close to one hundred degrees during the Coachella Festival, not ideal for selling vinyl records. Kurtz took Fold's idea of a record store on site to Steve Duncan and Brian Faber, the two guys who ran Zia Records out of Phoenix. Duncan, who had at the time recently left Rasputin (which hosted Metallica on RSD the previous year) for Zia, remembers the Coachella opportunity.

> "The thought of creating a remote record store in the middle of the desert was terrifying. The drive to Coachella from Phoenix takes just over three hours. The economy was tanking and the idea of risking a bunch of money and resources sounded insane. Making Record Store Day a success was a huge reason for our participation. The branding opportunity for Record Store Day, and of course Zia Records seemed like a worthy gamble. Southern California has a huge music community and having a store onsite to serve them was in our opinion important. We ended up doing a five-year (2009-2013) run and without a doubt the gamble paid off."

Duncan and Faber pondered the concept and came back with drawings for constructing a record store on site, complete with a refrigerated room for storing records, so that when the fan purchased their Record Store Day releases, they could leave it with Zia and pick them up when it was time to leave the festival. Every person who attended was given a guide, and it pointed fans to discover the on-site record store, celebrate Record Store Day, as well as meet and get autographs from many of the artists who performed at Coachella those first few years.

They included: Ghostland Observatory, Steve Aoki, The Aggrolites, Cage the Elephant, Band of Horses, Atmosphere, Amanda Palmer, Ida Maria, Peter, Bjorn & John, Lyke Li, The Horrors, Gaslight Anthem, Superchunk, Fucked Up, Peanutbutter Wolf, Booker T & the DBT's, Thenewno2, Passion Pit, P.O.S., LCD Soundsystem, Deadmau5, LaRoux, The Avett Brothers, DJ Lance Rock, DEVO, Yeasayer, Ra Ra Roit, Dillinger Escape Plan, Sleigh Bells, Baroness, Wale, MGMT, The Gossip, Diplo/Major Lazer, John Waters, Charlotte Gainsbourg, Muthmath, Matt & Kim, King Khan, Florence + The Machine, Little Boots, Miike Snow, Mayer Hawthorne, Local Natives, Soft Pack, Pavement, Shooter Jennings, Temper Trap, and Band of Skulls.

In hindsight, Kurtz realizes the importance of the Coachella store and all of those artist events. "It was an out of the blue innovation and changed everything. Zia and Record Store Day ran an amazing record store with non-stop artist events inside the store. And the effect on Record Store Day and vinyl itself can't be over-exaggerated."

Unbeknownst to almost everyone at the time, about a quarter the units sold on Record Store Day on April 18, 2009, were sold at Zia's Coachella record store. Kurtz now reveals. "By expanding with Zia's on-site store, we were able to artificially pump up the early vinyl numbers and simultaneously reach attending music fans from around the world. This helped us to get more and more stores and artists involved and set into motion Kurtz working on Record Store Day globally."

The actual beginning of Record Store Day officially going international and creating the first global "street date" started with the independently owned, Canadian chain of stores called Sunrise Records joining the Department of Record Stores coalition. There was no road map of where everything was heading at the time, but Michael Kurtz intuitively knew that to compete with international corporations like Amazon and Apple Computer's iTunes, independent record stores had to look past boundaries. Luckily, he found a like-minded business partner with Tim Baker, the guy who ran Sunrise. Together, they built the template for working beyond borders. Recalls Kurtz of their first encounter:

"Tim is this bigger-than-life person, known to rub people the wrong way when he thought they weren't being clear-headed about business. Underneath that gruff exterior, and all that tattooed skin, lies a real music fan with deep passion for the music business."

So when it came time to take RSD international, Canada's Sunrise Records was first in line. The UK was next on the list after the success of the first Record Store Day in 2008. Record Store Day provided Bull Moose's Chris Brown with some funding to help with his travels across the Atlantic for the first meeting with Rough Trade in London. It was fairly informal but set the stage for friendly discussions that led to Michael Kurtz flying over to the UK in response from emails he was getting from various people in Europe who wanted to discuss the possibility of joining the party. Kurtz's idea was simple: if you want to organize Record Store Day in your country then you have to abide by the same rules as the US stores, encourage in-store celebrations, and sell the Record Store Day exclusives at a fair price and at the same time as everyone else around the world.

London Calling

In March 2009, Kurtz accidentally bumped into English singer-songwriter Billy Bragg at the Austin, Texas, airport, following the annual music industry festival South By Southwest. Kurtz recognized Bragg, who had just read about the forthcoming RSD concept in a British magazine, *Mojo*. With less than a month to go, nothing could be organized officially, but Kurtz asked Bragg if he would consider playing at a record store on Record Store Day somewhere in England.

At the time, the British market also suffered from the same trends that hampered the US. HMV was the last big chain standing. A few years earlier, the flagship Virgin Megastore had left Oxford Street, as well as elsewhere throughout the country, and Tower Records' massive outpost on Piccadilly Circus was a recent memory.

In a reverse expansion move that ultimately failed, the American chain Borders closed forty-one UK superstores in 2009. Much as in the US, Britain's indie shops soldiered on, but the closures were alarming.

Spencer Hickman, who managed the 15,000-square-foot Rough Trade store off East London's historic Brick Lane, also read about RSD and was intrigued by the possibilities. He had tried to organize a coalition similar to CIMS or DORS, but to no avail. "We just couldn't do it. It was painfully obvious that we had fifteen stores with different agendas," he said, expressing envy that the American stores could join forces with a unified message to form three coalitions, let alone one, to gain their buying power. A few British stores endorsed an effort similar to RSD, for which they had a logo designed and put up a less than impressive website. "It just failed miserably."

Hickman eventually gained RSD's attention across the pond after sending Michael and Carrie an email. "I didn't know them. I asked, 'What's the deal here? Can we get involved?' And they just wrote back to me saying, 'Oh, yeah, we'd love for the UK to be involved.'" After getting the blessing from RSD USA, Hickman reached out to six indie stores with whom he was friendly, and they all liked what they heard, with one objection: "A lot of Brits fiercely proud of being British were like, 'We're not a "store"; we're a "shop."'" Hickman pointed out that "Record Store Day" sounds way better than "Record Shop Day." And it does.

Record shops throughout Britain, including Rough Trade's 6,000-square-foot West London store, on April 18, 2009, brought live music to their customers. "It was a celebration," Hickman adds, noting that the local and national media picked up the story. "We had packed stores all day, a ton of bands came through, a ton of people came through. It was suddenly a realization that even without the product people wanted, people were into the fact that they could come and just celebrate that culture with like-minded individuals.

It wasn't necessarily just about vinyl; it was about what the store embodies, what it means."

Hickman has no doubt that Record Store Day helped revive all the participating stores' fortunes, marveling at "this thing that it is today." He adds that Rough Trade would have survived without RSD, fueled by its strong brand and history in the UK, already weathering a lot of storms. That history includes being owned by the venerable Rough Trade label, which is now part of the venerable Beggars Group of independent labels, also including 4AD and Young Turks. Beggars founder and chairman Martin Mills (his Rough Trade store predated the labels) wanted to join up, and in fact, he notes its American label operation was among the first to participate in the US in 2008.

> "When I first heard of [RSD] it sounded like a great idea, and it's continued to be a great idea. Certainly as a shop owner, as well as a label owner, I know what a difference it makes to your numbers. [RSD expanding beyond the US] was kind of a no-brainer idea once we and the template have been drawn up."

In 2010, exclusive UK releases for RSD "started to flow," making it easier for Hickman to "galvanize other stores to be involved. It kind of grew from there, really."

After six years of being the UK point person for Record Store Day, Hickman took on the responsibility of finding a US retail location for Rough Trade, which turned out to be in Brooklyn, New York. Even though he was supposed to manage the American store in 2010, Hickman decided to leave Rough Trade completely and central London, launching a label, Death Waltz, which reissues obscure movie and TV soundtracks on vinyl. Death Waltz was acquired in 2015 by Mondo, for whom he currently works, and Hickman separately owns a tiny record shop called Transmission in Margate, on England's southern coast. For RSD, Death Waltz's seven-inch singles to date include for *Star Trek, The Addams Family, Twilight Zone, Outer Limits*, and *Alfred Hitchcock Presents.*

Hickman admits that an interview he gave to the online publication Quietus, acknowledging criticisms that UK record stores levied against Record Store Day, were not well received by some of its cofounders. He knew it was time to relinquish the RSD responsibility, for which he notes he was not paid. He turned over the RSD task to the UK trade organization, the Entertainment Retailers Association (ERA). Responsibilities included liaison with the American organization, line up the British shops, as well as review and coordinate RSD releases from British labels.

"It wasn't really until the third or fourth year where there was a core of thirty or so shops that were [already] involved with ERA," explains Kim Bayley, ERA's chief executive. "I think it got to a level where it was unmanageable for one person from one shop to coordinate, at which point Spencer kind of introduced Michael [Kurtz] to ERA. The first few years we did it, it was still very informal. A lot of the shops did the PR and a lot of the admin, and we just kind of facilitated the back end, and it grew from there. Once we got to more than fifty shops plus, [ERA] started driving forward the PR for Record Store Day as an entity with websites and everything else." Currently, about 130 UK stores sell new vinyl, among the 400 total that sell mostly used records.

A watershed RSD release for the UK market was one thousand copies of a newly recorded Blur single "Fool's Day" on April 17, 2010, containing a newly recorded song, which wasn't otherwise available, marking the band's first new music since 2003. "I think after that the rest is history," comments Megan Page, ERA's day-to-day RSD coordinator.

"That Blur record really got headlines from the news media, people queuing up around the block. That really started what we now know is Record Store Day in terms of the chaos around people wanting these releases

Page points out that most of the RSD titles for the UK market have been "smaller releases," but Blur was among the first major British artists who "kind of stuck a fork in the ground and said, 'We support and love record stores.'"

The British music press and media embraced the RSD story, and as Bayley points out, "That's the advantage of being a smaller country, it's quite easy for ERA to have those personal communications."

France Wants In Too

As with Spencer Hickman, over in France, David Godevais was already doing his part to keep vinyl alive years before RSD came along. In 2002, he founded "CALIF" (Club Action des Labels et des Disquaires Independants Francais) because he was alarmed by indie music shops getting squeezed out of the business by the big Walmart-like chains. Previously, Godevais headed an independent jazz label association, as well as his own label. He studied composition and orchestration at CIM jazz school, the French equivalent to the Berklee School of Music in Boston, Mass. Godevais had also been a cultural advisor for nearly three years (2017-2020) and in the cabinet of the city of Paris Mayor Anne Hidalgo, who David has known and been close to since 2004. For David—and apparently the French government—selling records is not merely a commercial transaction. He explains:

> "When you go and buy music, it is a completely different experience at a record store than if you go to a supermarket to buy a record because of the person who runs a record store who's passionate. You buy [the shop owner's] passion for music. And it's also socializing. If you go to your local butcher and buy meat, you can talk about recipes and preparation. [Record stores] are a place where you can talk with people, bring your imagination, discuss what you like, get advice even if you don't agree with them. We can't leave

record sales to a supermarket or a massive shop where you can buy chairs, food, or whatever."

At the time, France was coming to grips with the notion that bookstores needed to be preserved and subsidized if need be. Using that precedent, Godevais saw an opportunity to approach the government to also save specialized music stores as a cultural mission. "I went to see the government and said, 'Okay, I need some financial backing from you.'" Demonstrating his immense power of persuasion, David came away with a government commitment to pay six months of rent in advance for any new record store that is opening, a third of the rent for the second year, and a quarter of the rent the fourth year, with a cap at 10,000 euros per year. As a result of the initiative, 150 new record stores opened in France, points out Godevais.

> "I suggested [to the government] this is the way you can build a company because otherwise many would need to close. If you can't pay the rent you're dead. [The government] understood they were [already] helping a lot of bookstores. I tried to be convincing [with the rationale] every time you bring one euro to CALIF then take three euros back just on VAT. They said, 'Yeah, why not?'"

The French government understood they were investing in the future, and Godevais shortly after proved that their money was not being wasted and that indie record shops were a real cottage industry that could become an economic boon.

Meanwhile, store beneficiaries of these considerable tax breaks saw the value in joining CALIF because members saw Godevais's effectiveness in being an advocate for their cause, he notes.

Fast forward to mid-2010. Record Store Day has already happened three times in the US, twice in the UK (but only once with RSD product). Godevais and Kurtz hadn't yet crossed paths. "I was trying to contact Michael for months, looking for his email address.

By August or September [2010], I finally reached him and explained what I was doing. Then [Kurtz] called me, and said maybe we could join together because what you're doing is great." Michael invited David to join him and representatives from Spain, the Netherlands, and the UK in London. Godevais bought a one-day train ticket.

"I see Michael at nine o'clock in the morning in the hotel lobby. He says, 'Okay, follow me.' I follow him to another room. There are about twenty people sitting there. He tells me to sit. I didn't understand [what was going on] because I thought we were supposed to have a one-on-one meeting. Everybody presents themselves, including Record Store Day representatives of the United Kingdom, The Netherlands, and Spain. The English labels were there. And it comes to me, and Michael introduces me, 'Oh, this is David. He's gonna do the French Record Store Day.' The British are very pragmatic. They ask, 'How many record stores are going to participate?' I didn't have a clue. So I say [totally bluffing], 'About one hundred!'"

The Frenchman's answer apparently satisfied the Brits, even though Godevais made up the number. The Brits pledge four hundred shops, "and then the meeting stops." David meets Spencer Hickman, introduced as "the big guy working at Rough Trade."

Luckily, Godevais was already discussing with his French government contact about doing an indie store promotion for France, not considering it could be part of a wider international effort. David's brain waves are spinning, "Well this could work," telling himself, "I need to stay in London a few more days."

David then tells Michael and Spencer, "In France, I am not going to call it 'Record Store Day' because it doesn't mean anything [to French] people. The people who work in a record store are called a 'disquaire.' I would like to call it 'Disquaire Day.' They look at me, and they say, 'It sounds like D-Day. Yes, you could do that.'"

David tagged along with Michael and Spencer to meetings with EMI and Universal (which hadn't yet merged at this point), "which was brilliant." He anticipated potential releases from the likes of Gorillaz and David Bowie for Disquaire Day releases that coming spring.

So Godevais had "three months to build everything," and deployed a similar approach with the distribution companies and the major labels to get exclusive French product for Disquaire Day. For CALIF, he's already had some dealings with them over obtaining rebates or discounts for indie stores to make them more competitive with what the big chains would pay, much in the same way the American coalitions—pre-RSD—had to create their own exclusive releases.

CALIF's communications with the major labels were initially met with derision. "The majors—Universal, Sony, and Warner—were against [providing exclusive Disquaire Day releases], telling me, 'Don't mess up the deal we have with Fnac,' the French equivalent of HMV."

Godevais tried to reason with the majors that they would benefit by participating in Disquaire Day. "Back in Paris, [label] people in France were saying, 'We're not sure,' and I said, 'Well, tell them just go fuck themselves because we will get them from the UK. We're going to sell [the records] anyway.'"

As an association, CALIF didn't have existing sales accounts with the majors, similar to the same hindrance that the pre-RSD coalitions had when they initially procured exclusive product for their indie stores. "As it turned out, almost none of the CALIF members possessed open accounts with the majors, so [the plan] couldn't work," David realized. CALIF had no choice but to start a distribution company, much in the same way Don VanCleave did with CIMS' JunketBoy. "Otherwise, the record stores won't have [RSD releases]."

In an email explaining the situation to CALIF members, ninety-six of them replied they wanted to be part of Disquaire Day, "and I was saying one hundred to the British," he laughs. Eight additional video stores pledged to participate in the first French RSD, putting Godevais over the top of his totally made-up prediction.

Independent labels agreed to provide seven pieces of special product sung in French, whereas the majors came up with twenty-three releases of either American or British artists singing in English, but the latter batch didn't come easily, even from the Paris offices of the majors. For example, a Warner exec agreed to "get some stuff," but then reversed himself upon learning there was no existing account. "Then I went to see EMI, and they say, 'Yeah, why not?' But an EMI general manager found out about the Gorillaz RSD release and tells my friend, Andres Garrido, who used to work at EMI: 'Well, sorry, but we won't be able to give you that' [because it was destined to go to Fnac as an exclusive]. I then emailed Michael [Kurtz] to confirm that Gorillaz is a Record Store Day exclusive, and let him know of EMI's plan to give it to the chain instead. I was copied on an email going from the US to the UK saying, 'There seems to be a problem about Gorillaz being an exclusive.' The next day the guy from EMI says, 'Oh, sorry, we didn't understand. We're gonna sell it to you on Monday,' and five minutes later, he calls back and says, 'Well, there was a misunderstanding, the Record Store Day stuff is for you."

Godevais then meets with Universal France, where he learns of planned RSD releases for Sonic Youth, Rolling Stones with an unreleased track (the same one that the UK was getting), and a live Nirvana.

> "I had a friend who was in charge at Universal for all things international. He organized a meeting for me, with the head of sales, who said, 'Well, we're going to sell that to Fnac,' to which I replied, 'I don't think you're going to do that. I think you should have a talk with the Universal American people.' He says, 'We're Universal France. We don't care about Universal US. We do our own stuff.' And I say, 'Yeah, you do your own stuff' and leave the office. Thirty minutes later, I get a call from the Universal guy, 'Yeah, well, there was some kind of misunderstanding.'"

Godevais knew he still needed to get out the word about Disquaire Day, and that might cost some money, which he probably could get from the government since the Minister of Culture offered to help. So his friend Andres, who used to work at EMI, found out that it would cost 40,000 Euros to insert 100,000 copies of a sixteen-page Disquaire Day supplement in France's leading culture magazine *Inrockuptibles*, published on the previous Wednesday.

David's initial reaction: "I don't have that kind of money," to which Andres says, "Well, go find it because we need it." Much to his surprise, the government official initially agrees. But there was a problem when he went to pick up the check. "She tells me, 'The big boss is not convinced we should give you this money. You need to explain why you need so much money.'"

Godevais implores that Disquaire Day will not work without this media buy, and he reminds her of how the government's previous investment into what these indies stores were doing over the past five years was already paying dividends in tax money that otherwise would not be in their coffers.

"She says, 'I'm gonna call the magazine and call them a 'thief' because forty thousand euros is way too much.'" Even though the publisher would not budge on the price, she agrees to write to the check after an hour of discussion because of David's insistence the supplement is still a worthwhile expense since "everyone in the French media reads it." The magazine produced free Disquaires Day publicity, such as an interview Godevais did on an influential national radio show, the equivalent of the UK's BBC One.

Content in the French-language supplement included articles about the origins of Disquaire Day, a list of the 104 participating stores in France, as well as articles about the thirty special releases. That next Saturday, "they made money like they never had done before," David remembers. "They didn't expect to have so many people coming to indie record stores. They never had seen that many customers in their life and sold so many records. It was crazy. It was kind of an adventure, you know?"

In 2011, Godevais, Kurtz and Spencer Hickman met up for coffee in New York, trading notes on their various inroads into getting respect for indie stores when it previously seemed impossible. David relayed to them some of the stories told above.

"Spencer looks at me and says, 'David, you're a fucking Viking. You go with an axe and you smash everybody.'"

Most importantly, Disquaire Day was now firmly established, as evidenced by the growth in participating stores from 100 to 160, an increase in Record Store Day releases, and expanding turntable sales that rippled through the economy. Finally, the majors started opening sales accounts for indie stores.

Dutch RSD Leads to a Romantic Partnership

When Michael Kurtz first met Marlein Parlevliet at the London meeting, he was impressed. "Marlein had a lot of confidence and she knew everything about music and record stores to the point I left our meeting convinced she had actually been born in an record store." In reality, Marlein did grow up in a record store family in The Netherlands. Her father, Hans Parlevliet, created the venerable brick-and-mortar chain Velvet Music that expanded to fifteen stores throughout the country. All the Parlevliets worked there, "everybody, the whole family, sister, brother…." Since Marlein was fourteen years old, she worked in the shop and learned all aspects of the business, but her family's elders prohibited her from working behind the counter because she mispronounced "Dylan."

Eight years later, a Velvet Music fan sent the store an email about this going on called Record Store Day. Marlein thought to herself, "Why are we not celebrating this? Hey, we need to do this in the Netherlands too!" As it turned out, two other stores already were

RSD stores. "I was like, we have to make this international thing in Europe as well," she explains.

Despite her youth, she was her own woman, and had enough gumption to convince the Dutch record stores they should band together for everyone's benefit on the RSD initiative that already made waves across the Atlantic, as well as in Great Britain. The Netherlands had the opportunity to become the third RSD country.

Faced with the double challenge of being born with a famous surname and working in a business dominated by men, Parlevliet could never be accused of playing the nepotism card. She asked the Dutch record store association NVR, "Hey, can I organize this for you?" The response: "Yeah, well, okay." Her mission was to sign up its membership of fifty stores to participate in the internationally recognized Record Store Day.

"I had to convince all the stores. I had to convince the media. I had to convince the artists. So because [RSD] was not really a big thing yet in Europe, it was quite difficult to convince everybody, especially because I was a twenty-two-year-old girl. A lot of record stores were like, 'She doesn't know anything about vinyl,' giving me some self-doubt if I was just wasting my time. I really had to fight for my place." Her knowledge of the business, as well as music, eventually satisfied any concerns. One skeptical Dutch journalist, eight years older than she at the time, wrote for the biggest online music journal in the Netherlands. "He was always writing shit about record stores." But he initially was very skeptical of the RSD mission and wasn't buying her story. "I realized I needed to convince him that record stores are a lot of fun. So we kept talking and talking and talking about it. Now he's my partner, the father of my child, and we live together."

She also had some non-Velvet work experience at a television studio on a popular program in the Netherlands, giving her more confidence, as well as a built-in platform to enlist artists to endorse the Dutch edition of RSD. "Every day they had live musicians in our studio. They then would play for free in our stores," remembers

Congratulations

Record Store Day
Los Angeles
April 19, 2014

WHEREAS, THROUGHOUT MUSIC HISTORY, RECORD STORES HAVE BEEN AN IMPORTANT PART OF OUR LIVES. MORE THAN JUST TO GET THE LATEST HITS FROM YOUR FAVORITE MUSICIANS, THEY PROVIDE A VENUE TO EXPAND YOUR MUSICAL HORIZONS AND LEARN ABOUT OTHER CULTURES, SUPPORT ARTISTS AND THE MUSIC INDUSTRY, AND DEBATE WHICH IS THE BEST GUITAR SOLO OF ALL TIME; AND

WHEREAS, INDEPENDENT RECORD STORES HAVE BEEN CRUCIAL IN LAUNCHING THE CAREERS OF SOME OF THE BIGGEST NAMES AND TRENDS IN MUSIC. BUT IN RECENT YEARS, THE PROLIFERATION OF FREE MUSIC ON THE INTERNET HAS THREATENED THIS VITAL INDUSTRY MORE AND MORE; AND

WHEREAS, 'RECORD STORE DAY' IS AN IMPORTANT OPPORTUNITY TO SUPPORT LOCAL BUSINESSES AND MUSICIANS, AND THE MUSIC INDUSTRY IN GENERAL. MORE THAN 1000 STORES WORLDWIDE-INCLUDING AMOEBA IN HOLLYWOOD TO STORES IN NEW YORK CITY, LONDON, PARIS, TOKYO AND BEYOND - WILL PARTICIPATE IN THE 2014 EVENT; AND

WHEREAS, MUSIC LOVERS ENJOY THE OPPORTUNITY TO GET THEIR HANDS ON SOME RARE RECORDINGS AND LIMITED EDITION ITEMS, MEET SOME OF THEIR FAVORITE MUSICIANS, AND EXPERIENCE THIS YEARLY CELEBRATION OF MUSICAL COMMUNITY:

NOW THEREFORE, I ERIC GARCETTI, AS MAYOR OF THE CITY OF LOS ANGELES, AND ON BEHALF OF IS RESIDENTS, DO HEREBY RECOGNIZE APRIL 19, 2014 AS RECORD STORE DAY, IN LOS ANGELES. I ENCOURAGE EVERYONE TO VISIT YOUR LOCAL RECORD STORE, PICK UP A CD, AN LP, OR A DVD AND DO YOUR PART TO KEEP THE RECORD STORE INDUSTRY ROCKING AND ROLLING IN THE YEARS TO COME.

March 6, 2014

ERIC GARCETTI
Mayor

Los Angeles Mayor Garcetti's 2014 declaration celebrating Record Store Day

Photo courtesy of Record Store Day

Michael Kurtz and Jack White at the Detroit Making Vinyl Conference
Photo courtesy of Making Vinyl

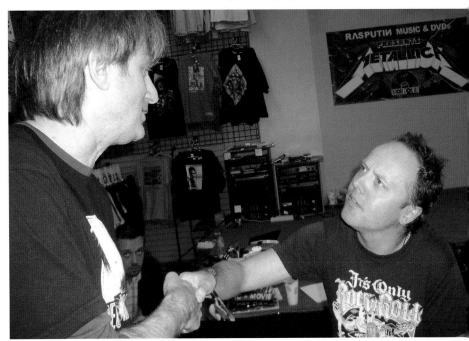

Michael Kurtz shakes the hand of Lars Ulrich at the launch of Record Store Day
in their hometown store of Rasputin Music.
Photo courtesy of Fawn Goodman

The Doors' drummer John Densmore and Public Enemy's Chuck D celebrating
Record Store Day at Amoeba, Hollywood, CA

Photo courtesy of Record Store Day

The team behind Record Store Day: Michael Kurtz and Carrie Colliton

Photo courtesy of Record Store Day

The Decemberists' violinist Sara Watkins lets a young fan play her instrument
at Bull Moose on Record Store Day

Photo courtesy of Matthew Robbins

Mayday Parade fans celebrating Record Store Day at Vintage Vinyl, NJ

Photo courtesy of Record Store Day

The Foo Fighters celebrating Record Store Day at Fingerprints, Long Beach, CA

Photos courtesy of John Gilhooley

Brandi Carlile before her performance at Easy Street Records
Photo courtesy of Hannah Hanseroth

Don VanCleave holding court after Pearl Jam recorded at Easy Street Records. L to R: Cameron
Crowe, Eddie Vedder, Don VanCleave, Nancy Wilson, Jim James, John Doe, and Mike Creedy
Photo courtesy of Bootsy Holler

Lolo Reskin and Iggy Pop
celebrating Iggy's birthday at
Sweat Records in Miami, FL, on
Record Store Day
Photo courtesy of teajayphoto

St. Vincent, Record Store Day
2017 Ambassador
Photo courtesy of Record Store Day

Marlein, estimating some 160 mostly Dutch artists performed, although a few A-list British artists, such as 10cc, also did in-stores.

Typically about ten Dutch artists contribute records for RSD. Getting American and British records for RSD wasn't so easy. "The USA is such a big market. The UK is such a big market. Nobody gives a shit about the Netherlands. It's not a big country. So we received the leftovers for the first three or four years. We needed to show the record companies that Holland is also important, and we also wanted to have some of the nicest best-selling titles," she explains. "So that's why I went to Germany and Belgium and other European countries to get the quantities [required to be taken more seriously]."

When she was getting the Dutch RSD off the ground, she visited Spencer Hickman in London. "He was one of my best friends in the Record Store Day community. He's such a good entrepreneur." Also helpful to her was Jan Koepke, the RSD coordinator in Germany, Austria, and Switzerland, as being particularly helpful in getting the Europeans better recognition.

"First we take Manhattan, then Berlin"—Leonard Cohen

Record industry veteran Jan Koepke, who's based in Hamburg, Germany, currently manages Record Store Day in three countries: Germany, Austria, and Switzerland. How did he assume such responsibilities?

> "This was in 2011. I was hanging out at the Haldern Pop Festival, when Michael Schuster (who is running Cargo Records Germany, one of the very early RSD supporters in continental Europe) came up to me and asked if I could imagine to represent and organize Record Store Day here in Germany, as well as in Austria and Switzerland. We knew each other for quite a while, as I have run my own label and PR company since 2001. So I took the challenge—without any concrete idea how we shall finance the project. It was

Michael Kurtz and his Dutch RSD colleagues who were very helpful with advice on acquiring first sponsorships and sharing experience on how to collaborate with the industry on one side and the shops on the other side."

Koepke first met Kurtz in 2013 in New York City when all international RSD coordinators met in New York for an "international RSD get together" with a bunch of roundtable talks and visits with the record companies. Not to mention, the whiskey bars of Manhattan. "We did this a few years in a row, and I enjoyed these get-togethers a lot. Getting to know the people behind RSD in Europe and America was extremely helpful and inspiring and not to forget to mention that we all had really great times together in New York. Michael and Carrie had been great hosts for us!"

The reason why Koepke and his German team also look after RSD in Switzerland and Austria as well is that the labels and distributors traditionally treat the three (German-speaking) countries as one sales territory called the "GSA" territory. "I learned that this abbreviation is not common knowledge in the music biz in the States. Speaking the same language is probably the origin and reason why GSA is used in contracts and marketing plans for record releases," shares Koepke.

Koepke notes German is the only language in Germany and Austria, and also spoken in major parts of Switzerland, which, although it is very small, is separated by four different language regions. Beside the German region, there is a French sector, an Italian speaking one, and the Rhaeto-Romanic dialect spoken in southeastern Switzerland, which had been the former Roman province of Rhaetia.

Koepke continues to closely coordinate the GSA's efforts with other European countries. "Especially with those who I had the pleasure to meet up with personally, we have good connections among each other to solve things quickly and friendly in the event of unauthorized release leaks or upfront online offers in any of the countries. Still, each country within Europe is very individual and different, in regard to distribution, especially for the culture and history of the indie record store world, as well as the culture." As of January 2021, 247 German, Swiss, and Austrian stores were committed to participate in RSD's June and July 2021 drops, but Koepke expects a few new requests.

As far as the actual music contained on RSD releases distributed to GSA stores, a bunch of German domestic releases every year, in German as well as in English lyrics. "This is indeed a main topic—or personal wish for me—to find a way to increase this number sustainably," Koepke admits. "The majority of the RSD exclusives are released by internationally active labels that sell their releases worldwide. So, with a few exceptions like Rammstein or Einstürzende Neubauten—just to name two iconic artists—it is easy to imagine that economically a small number of a limited RSD items to be sold in one market only, is less attractive for labels and artist than any regular release."

Koepke admits his PR background has helped a lot in gaining publicity for RSD. "My team at popup-records is providing PR services for many international labels (e.g., Caroline International, Cooking Vinyl, The Orchard, Secretly Canadian, just to name a few), so we speak to the music journalists on a daily basis—in all fields of media, if it is radio hosts, blog writers, *Rolling Stone* editors or TV producers, a very broad and diverse media landscape in our territory. We have our regular topics with these guys and Record Store Day is definitely an annual priority. Besides broader mass media outlets, I am very happy that we have *MINT* magazine—extremely popular in the German-speaking region—as our media partner on our side for many years, which has been an enthusiastic supporter of Record Store Day."

RSD resurrects Japan's Mini Record Player

When Michael Kurtz thinks about Japan, the words innovation, reverence, and quality come to mind. "When all vinyl collectors think of high quality, they think of Japanese pressings. There is a mystique to them."

In 2018, Kurtz was invited to come to Japan to meet with industry leaders, make the rounds with the media, and to help take Record Store Day to the next level. While in the country, Kurtz met with CEO/President Katsuharu Hagiwara from Toyo Kasei, Japan's oldest vinyl manufacturing plant and the company that runs Record Store Day in Japan. Kurtz took several tours of the plant, leaving him impressed. "The closest comparison I can make to Toyo Kasei is Jack White's Third Man plant in Detroit. They both are state-of-the-art facilities, beautiful to look at and seamless in their operations." At the end of those three days of doing media meetings, Mr. Hagiwara showed Kurtz a Bandai three-inch turntable, originally made in the 1960s to play music made for Japanese anime and said, "I'd like for you to bring this back to life and find somebody to manufacture the mini turntables so we can make three-inch records again." Kurtz didn't need convincing.

"The packaging on the three-inch records is pretty stunning, and they make a perfect piece for fans, so I said, 'I'll try, it's a really cool thing. I love it; it's a lot of fun, and it definitely puts a big smile on my face.'"

Kurtz brought the Bandai version back to the US and showed it to Record Store Day's long-term turntable partner Crosley.

"Crosley takes a lot of heat for manufacturing the early suitcase style turntables," Kurtz acknowledges. "But those early turntables are what helped turn millions of music fans into vinyl buyers. Beyond that they are innovators, and saw the potential that Mr. Hagiwara presented to Record Store Day."

Kurtz also learned that Jack White had been fooling around with the idea of a mini record player. "Jack had earlier discovered the Bandai three-inch records on a tour of Japan," Kurtz notes. "He made the three-inch records when he got back to the United States and then discovered that there were no turntables to play them. "So I brought the RSD concept to Third Man Records' Ben Blackwell, who took it to Jack, and he said, 'This is awesome.' He's always wanted to do it."

"The resurrection of the abandoned three-inch format is an unlikely set of circumstances," comments Scott Bingaman, owner and president of St. Louis, Missouri-based Deer Park Distributors.

Each one-sided single contains one song and a collector's poster. "The idea is that it's supposed to be a fan piece." Eclectic record content came from the likes of the Foo Fighters, Sun Records, Post Malone, Bad Religion, Jack White, Czarface/MF Doom, and the Beastie Boys, of the more than twenty mini-record artists available.

CHAPTER EIGHT

The Under Assistant West Coast Promotion Man

"If it weren't for Michael, Carrie, and Record Store Day, there would be no physical music business left."
—Donna Ross, Concord Music Group

[2008–2011: Indie labels including Beggars, Third Man, Epitaph, Concord, Sundazed, Resonance, and ORG explain how Record Store Day improved their fortunes with vinyl.]

IN 2009, EAGLES OF DEATH Metal's Jesse "Boots Electric" Hughes proposed that Record Store Day anoint an Ambassador yearly to, as Kurtz put it, "claim the mantle of greatness that conveys the majesty of the artist events and amazing array of releases made on the world's only holiday devoted to music." Hughes was the first, and shortly thereafter, Queen of the Stone Age's Josh Homme announced he would be the second. Then, on *Saturday Night Live's* April 17, 2010, edition of "Weekend Update," Seth Meyers quipped "Today is Record Store Day, a day to celebrate your local record store. So head down there to get your Jamba Juice now."

Carrie Colliton flipped on the show live to decompress after a very long Year Three RSD. "My jaw was on the floor. We were made fun of by *Saturday Night Live*, but who cares? That's even better than them being nice about it. I think, 'Hey, we were a joke on *Weekend Update*.'"

CIMS' Andrea Paschal also watched it live, and realized that RSD had arrived. "That was the moment the little light bulb went off in my head, 'Other people know about it now.' It was very cool watching the switch from just being with your friends at drinks, 'What are you guys working on?' to seeing them be excited about the things they wanted to get for Record Store Day." Kurtz thought it was cool that the SNL researchers apparently picked up on the zeitgeist brewing even if it was in jest.

Just within the first few years, Record Store Day had reached over a million fans globally visiting record stores mostly driven by the special releases from the likes of Bruce Springsteen, the Rolling Stones, the Beatles, R.E.M., Blur, among others. The Record Store Day Coachella store held special events with Father John Misty, Foals, Tegan and Sara, Alt-J, The Wombats, Kurt Vile, Grimes, Aesop Roc, and the Dropkick Murphys.

RSD had received hundreds of millions of impressions from online, television, and print media; it was now time to get the indie record labels fully engaged.

Scores of indie labels were already pressing records mostly because their artists wanted to sell them on tour at the merchandise table. However, most indie labels took their time jumping into the RSD fray. It's expensive to press and distribute records and, to do it effectively you'd need to guarantee sell through to the stores. Eureka! Record Store Day solved the problem and "the indie labels changed their minds because they saw it working, and they saw stores being positive about it," Colliton explains.

Kurtz points out the sheer business created by RSD was undeniable and cemented acceptance.

"Until Record Store Day, I don't think there was really much of a business model for [vinyl]. But after Record Store Day, indie record labels started thinking, 'Hey, I can ship one thousand to two thousand copies of something and it is never coming back.' Then the light bulb went off, 'You know, that's gonna make us four thousand or five thousand dollars. All right, there's a business here. I'll do it.' And then you multiply that by ten, twenty, thirty, forty, or fifty titles, now you're talking a quarter of a million dollars in business. That's very healthy for a smaller record company."

Beggars, an RSD early adopter

When you look at the list of seventeen commercial titles that emerged in 2008 on the first Record Store Day, nearly a third of them came from Matador, a label distributed by The Beggars Group. Founded in London in 1973 initially as a retail operation, Beggars by 1977 put out its own music under various label imprints that now includes XL, 4AD, Rough Trade, Young Turks, Matador, and Beggars.

For Record Store Day, the Beggars labels, has released more than a hundred records since RSD's inception, of which about two-thirds titles were shared between the US and UK arms of the company. Matt Harmon, the president of the company's US branch, joined Beggars in 1996 a few years out of college. He remembers Beggars jumping on RSD in 2008.

"For the first year, it was a good mix: a Vampire Weekend single of 'A-Punk,' their biggest song; a single from a French band called The Teenagers; a Breeders single; a Stephen Malkmus ten-inch, two albums by Arthur Russell: *Love is Overtaking Me* and *Calling Out of Context*, as well as a twelve-inch EP tribute to the artist: *Four Songs by Arthur Russell*. Our labels sort of got together and picked those. We wanted to try a couple of things. We probably do between four to six every time. From the beginning, a big part of how we plan our Aprils has to do with Record Store Day."

Beggars Group founder and chairman Martin Mills, based in London, chimes in about RSD: "It was an obviously great idea that started in America, and it spread to the UK and other countries. It was kind of a no-brainer. The template had been drawn up."

Generally speaking, Mills believes only an independent label would allow their artists to present their music on vinyl in a deluxe manner that often is off-limits at a major. "The majors have very strict rules about how much you can spend on packaging. There's a natural tendency in the major world not to do nice packaging," says the London-based Mills, who provides a glimpse into label machinations:

> "And they tend to look at margins. Accountants have their say. So the independent world is obviously much more likely to do something just because it's great. The reason why artists and designers love vinyl, when compared to the CD, is that it's just a much better palette to paint on. And I think people got very frustrated with the limitations of the CD. And that's one of the reasons why people continue to love vinyl, as well as the sound, obviously. And we never stopped doing vinyl. In the days when we were manufacturing three formats, there was certainly a phase, we did less vinyl, and we tended to do vinyl for artists that cared about it, or who were appropriate to the bottom [line]. We were not doing it for everyone, but we are always doing it for a lot of releases. Then it started coming back, and now [vinyl] is the primary physical format for us."

How can Third Man top itself on RSD?

It's no accident that Third Man Records (TMR) timed the opening of its Nashville store on April 19, 2009. It was Record Store Day. The previous year for the first RSD Ben Blackwell, who runs Third Man Records, was in Ann Arbor, Michigan, with his band the Dirtbombs, who had a gig that night. "We just happened to walk into a record store and it was like, 'Oh, yeah, they're doing this Record

Store Day thing today.'" Ben reels off the artists who had titles for sale. "Yeah, it was like Vampire Weekend, Breeders, Steve Malkmus. I think they were mostly from Matador or Beggars label stuff. I got a copy of everything I wanted. And it was cool."

As previously noted, RSD's 2009 release list was considerably ramped up to eighty-five titles. Blackwell purposefully opened the brand-new Third Man Records store at 11:00 a.m., an hour after Grimey's (also in Nashville). "So the idea was me and [TMR's] Ben Swank were going to be first in line at Grimey's." They were armed with their picks including Sonic Youth and Jay Reatard in a split-single seven-inch 45 and a Jesus Lizard, seven-inch box set, among them. "I think those were the releases that we were after that time, and we brought them over here. We're a half mile from Grimey's and got all set up. We opened an hour later and a bunch of people from Grimey's came over to Third Man. It was a cool time." (Grimey's owner Doyle Davis was amused hearing from the author Blackwell's TMR store-opening story, which he did not previously know.)

Third Man sells only its own label's records in its store, so the 2009 RSD offerings were the debut of The Dead Weather seven-inch single of "Hang You from the Heavens"/"Are Friends Electric?" (Gary Numan cover), along with leftover tour merchandise from his boss (and uncle) Jack White. Blackwell admits that they learned retail as they went along.

"You know, stuff that had been sitting in Jack's White Stripes closet for ten years. So we had old t-shirts, some old singles and vinyl, it was just like a glorified merch table. We're handing out beer. It seems so quaint in hindsight that me and Swank never really ran a proper commercial business prior to that. We didn't have a cash register, or a credit card machine, we couldn't print receipts, it was cash only, no coin change. So everything was a solid dollar price. We didn't charge anyone sales tax. And we didn't keep track of what we sold. So I told the business office, 'Okay, here's six thousand dollars from the store.' They're like, 'What did you sell?' 'I don't know. Don't you just put it in the bank? Can't we just say this was a merch table for the day? Come on, help us out?' We got all squared away very shortly," Blackwell laughs.

While the TMR store still doesn't sell RSD releases other than its own, Third Man—the label—does provide RSD titles to other merchants every annual cycle. Sometimes things don't go as planned. For example, originally in commemoration of Third Man's three millionth record pressed, White was planning to send into space on Record Store Day 2012, a twelve-inch, gold-plated record containing the spoken-word musings of the astronomist Carl Sagan and scientist Stephen Hawking, called "A Glorious Dawn." "The Third Man single was originally supposed to be for Record Store Day," explains Blackwell.

"We were beholden to weather and wind patterns. We didn't get clearance from the FAA [to launch on April 21, 2012]. So if you go back and you look at our planning for Record Store Day, we had the space-surf rock band Man or Astro Man? playing. It all worked fine on its own, but it would have worked one thousand times better if we're launching a record into space that day."

In October, the Sagan record sailed into space 94,000 feet above the earth via a weather balloon and returned to earth hours later still spinning in a special construct record player. The project was years in the making. A seven-inch version of "A New Dawn" was first released by TMR in November 2009 with a B-side etching of the Voyager diagram, which was used in the RSD *The Voyager Golden Record* boxed-set release in 2017, winning Grammy and Making Vinyl packaging awards.

How do you beat sending a record into space? In 2013, the year Jack White became the official Record Store Day Ambassador, he recorded for RSD on April 20, 2013, a version of Loretta Lynn's classic country song "Coal Miner's Daughter" in Third Man Records' 1947 Voice-o-Graph recording booth, the only working one in the world. Neil Young also recorded a song there that day. "That's a pretty cool thing with Neil Young walking into your record store on Record Store Day," comments Blackwell. Young later recorded an entire album, *A Letter Home*, in the booth, sold as a TMR release for RSD the next year on April 20, 2014. For RSD 2013, also available was a tenth anniversary reissue of the White Stripes' *Elephant* on two LPs, consisting of one black-and-red colored disc and one white disc.

Epitaph & Sub Pop were early adopters

Before he and his label Epitaph became famous, Bad Religion lead guitarist Brett Gurewitz remembers hawking in 1981 his band's debut seven-inch single, named after the band, to indie record stores on consignment. An RSD limited edition of only 1,000 copies of Bad Religion's seven-inch EP, containing six tracks, was reissued in 2009 for the second Record Store Day.

The label was already on the vinyl bandwagon by the time Jon Strickland started working at Epitaph in 2004 for a twelve-year run. He's now with Sub Pop, another indie label with an indie record store mindset. Michael Kurtz lived near Epitaph's office in Los Angeles and Jon remembers having coffee regularly with him around the time he was seeking support for Record Store Day, and he was intrigued on reviving vinyl based on its recent past experience with the format.

"Epitaph had done good vinyl business all through the nineties. All of the Rancid and Pennywise, all of those kinds of bands, were selling really, really briskly on vinyl. I think that has something to do with punk rock. Punk stores were very old school and into vinyl. If you look on Discogs, a lot of the big surge of vinyl reissues and stuff really starts in the late aughts (just prior to Record Store Day), so there wasn't a ton of vinyl coming out. People were feeling like CDs were in trouble from digital. Big Box stores were starting to fold, making some indie stores nervous. But the Waterloos and the Music Millenniums were storied, had a real history in the community and were doing pretty good at the time. But small regional chains were cutting back stores."

A diminished retail revenue stream made labels nervous. Once Napster was unleashed and iTunes became a legal download alternative, Strickland observed the CMJ-type of customer, referring to the then influential College Media Journal, was more open to digital options and maybe abandoned vinyl sooner. "My sense starting in the mid-nineties was that Sub Pop stopped putting out a lot of stuff on vinyl, whereas Epitaph really kept going," Strickland explains. "And then suddenly, the bottom dropped out. And they were stuck with a lot of vinyl that just wasn't selling, and they built these fairly big reserves of vinyl. So when vinyl started coming back in the mid-aughts, Epitaph was much more gun-shy than a lot of the other indies because they had kind of gotten burned a little bit financially on vinyl going away."

Soon thereafter though, Epitaph and its sister label Anti-benefited from a series of really pretty big releases, such as Elliott Smith's *From the Basement on the Hill*, a couple of Tom Waits records, including *Real Gone*. "I think that one came out right after I started in 2004," Strickland remembers. "These were so great on vinyl because they were heritage artists. In my first two or three years at Epitaph, we realized this is real. We should get behind this."

Epitaph made posters to go into stores, which really loved them. "It wasn't selling any record, it was just a picture of Tom Waits, and just talking about record stores. A year or two year later, we did a poster with Neko Case, which was a big hit, too, because it had a particularly good picture of her sitting on the edge of a bathtub that I think was very popular with certain record store employees," Strickland remembers.

Epitaph also created specially designed Record Store Day T-shirts for Amoeba Records in Hollywood. "Epitaph would get local designers to kind of do cool Amoeba designs, and we started sponsoring those with an Epitaph or an Anti- logo on the back. We did that for the four or five years that I was there. It was kind of a cool way to celebrate record stores and the kind of things that happened in the record stores," notes Strickland, who joined Sub Pop, another indie label that embraced RSD and also figured prominently in the vinyl comeback.

Sub Pop's RSD strategy included creating an LP sampler of the label's artists and priced at five dollars and modeled after Warner Bros. Records' loss leaders double-LP samplers of the late 1960s and 1970s. Often labels provide free CD samplers for RSD. "I don't think there are a lot of people who were spending the money to do [samplers] on vinyl because that was a bit of a loss leader to do something like this. But a ton of indie labels did CD samplers."

Strickland is impressed with the recent explosion of reissue labels rallying around Record Store Day. "They really are digging the vaults. I see stuff coming out on vinyl for the first time, such as African music, some seventies Senegalese funk record. Somebody got a hold of the tapes, and they'd press up three thousand of them for Record Store Day. They'll sell because people are out looking for those kinds of weird, esoteric things. And that's a great discovery [for the RSD consumer]."

Kill Rock Stars by '09 all over it

Portia Sabin, currently president of MusicBiz, in 2006 took over the indie label Kill Rock Stars (KRS) that her husband Slim Moon launched in 1991 until September 2019 after running KRS for thirteen years. Heading the label gave Sabin an understanding of how important vinyl was to her artists and why they were enamored with the Record Store Day concept.

"Vinyl was everybody's preferred medium [over CD or cassette]. Over time, the cost of vinyl became so prohibitive, that [Moon] started putting out less and less vinyl. When I took over the label in 2006, we started doing vinyl again. There was this beginning, a strengthening, of the vinyl. Any indie artist wants to put out vinyl and that's a real problem, given the state of the industry now with the shift to digital music, because you just can't make back your investment anymore on a brand-new band on vinyl. It's a very difficult financial proposition for an untried band."

When KRS first heard about RSD, "we were totally all over it, thinking 'that's fantastic': independent labels always have had a tight relationship with indie retail. We were always wanting to do as much as we could with retail." But in 2008, KRS was having distribution issues. "It was chaos—so its RSD splash had to wait. In 2009, we did manage to make a Record Store Day split-seven inch for The Thermals and Thao & the Get Down Stay Down," explains Sabin, who signed both artists in 2008. "The Thermals already had a pretty successful album or two on Sub Pop. [The split single] was a great way to get some of our newer artists out there," Sabin explains.

"You have to make sure that the thing that you're giving them is really, really special," Sabin notes. "So that's how we played it. We did a big one in 2013 with an Elliott Smith seven-inch that was obviously gonna sell really well." She cites another example of a KRS release on RSD in 2015: The Decemberists' second album *Picaresque*, which had sold 250,000 copies on CD when it came out in 2002, a "ridiculous" sales figure for an indie label. "Those days are so far gone. I think we made like 5,000 units [of the RSD vinyl release], and they were gone in seconds."

Indie labels sometimes wonder if it always makes sense to focus on RSD when there are so many releases that it's hard to get noticed. Furthermore, only about half of what's submitted to RSD actually gets accepted.

As RSD grew in popularity, by 2016, [KRS] didn't [submit] anything," Sabin admits, noting there's no guarantee a label's release will get accepted. "We started thinking very carefully about what we were going to release for Record Store Day because we knew that it had to be something that people really wanted. In other words, I think when Record Store Day first started, we were like, 'Oh, this is a great way to introduce our young new hot artists.' And within a few years, it became, 'Oh shit, this is for our legacy artists.' This is for our special releases, as opposed to wasn't a discovery mechanism anymore."

But even though KRS pulled back on putting out RSD releases, its artists would often do in-store appearances at indie stores on Record Store Day. "That was always a big part of it," Sabin explains. "Anyone who was on tour, we definitely would help them, you know, hook them up with a record store to play. It is all about who's on tour, when, where, and what's happening," she says, citing KRS artists' schedule in 2017 when on RSD the supergroup Filthy Friends featuring Peter Buck (REM), Corin Tucker (Sleater-Kinney), and Scott McCoy (Young Fresh Fellows) and Bill Rieflin (Ministry). In 2017 RSD, a Filthy Friends seven-inch single, including a B-side cover version of Roxy Music's "Editions of You," was released because they were on tour.

Concord: "RSD almost like a money-printing machine"

The Concord Music Group harks back to 1973 when jazz guitarists Herb Ellis and Joe Pass recorded an album. Over the years, its owners included legendary TV impresario Norman Lear. For the past two decades, Concord has been in acquisition mode, acquiring the venerable catalogs of Fantasy/Prestige/Milestone/Riverside, Stax,

Telarc, Rounder, Vanguard, Sugar Hill, Varèse Sarabande, Vee-Jay, and Wind-up, cutting across genres. Recently, its vinyl releases included reissues by its Craft imprint and also new recordings from Lorna Vista.

Donna Ross, currently VP of sales for the Concord Music Group, which she joined three years ago, is in a good position to observe how Record Store Day changed labels' thinking, especially since she was present for the pivotal 2007 Noise in the Basement meeting when RSD was approved. At that point, Ross ran her own consultancy, after which she worked with the music marketing firm Ingrooves. For her, watching RSD grow has been a beautiful journey.

> "I don't think any of us would really have jobs in the physical world if it wasn't for Record Store Day. What they brought is greater than you can imagine, the excitement and specialness of creating this demand was so brilliant. [Before RSD] the whole industry was imploding on itself. CD [sales were declining dramatically], digital downloads just came in, streaming coming, and it was like over. Then out of nowhere, pops up this great demand for vinyl, and just the respect and the quality. Those early titles just sold out, and they were so collectible. Everyone put their blood and guts into the early days. Now kinda, it's almost like a money-printing machine. Now [RSD] is so well established and a trusted brand that if you just put it out there, people buy it. It's become so much bigger than they could have ever imagined. It's sustainable and global. Record Store Day raised the level of expectations. I don't think a box set like this (Chet Baker's *The Riverside Albums*, released in November 2020, a few weeks before RSD Black Friday) would have come out unless Record Store Day happened. You know how much it costs to make something like this? Would a label even have the guts to make something like that without really feeling the demand. Record Store Day

just created this renaissance. [Former Warner executive] Tom Whalley is Concord's chief music officer. His standard of vinyl is that it needs to be top quality, no more just cranking out crummy reissues. We care about mastering, care about the weight of the record, care about the artwork and packaging. It's just all part of the experience, that's what keeps people coming back."

RSD fit Omnivore's modus operandi

Omnivore Recordings, cofounded in 2011 by four former major label executives, began with a mission of putting out records that fell through the cracks and has since resulted in more than 400 releases, including perennial Record Store Day picks.

"From day one, Omnivore was set up to catch music that may fall by the wayside or get lost to time, and throw it into the future for others to find," explains Omnivore cofounder/co-owner Cheryl Pawelski. "It's no mistake that our first release in 2011 was a Record Store Day release: Big Star's *Third* (Test Pressing Edition) because obviously, there's a great story to that band and those recordings."

Two years after Omnivore's RSD first release, the label found another great record story in Three Hits, resurrecting a North Carolina band's 1985 EP that was initially released on Hib-Tone, the indie label that issued R.E.M's earliest home-made singles, including the 1981 breakthrough track "Radio Free Europe." Like R.E.M., Three Hits' early music was produced and engineered by Don Dixon at Drive-In Studio, where R.E.M. recorded its first four albums. Here's the interesting tie-in: Three Hits was co-founded by Michael Kurtz, his brother, Danny, and two friends, [Michael's future ex-wife] Sheila Valentine and Jim Biddell. Pawelski saw a correlation between R.E.M. and Three Hits on Hib-Tone, releasing limited-edition records, selling them to fans and in record stores.

"We were thrilled to be part of connecting those dots and telling that story. It was extra cool that R.E.M. also participated in the very first Record Store Day. I love the lines connecting the Record Store Day story across the eras, and we've been honored to be part of the continuum."

Speaking of his younger self, Kurtz says: "That was a person who really wanted to make it as an artist out of Boone, North Carolina." Almost embarrassed to answer why his former band's music made it onto an RSD release, Kurtz notes it was Omnivore's idea, not his. Three Hits rehearsed between the bins at Schoolkids Records, eventually touring up and down the East Coast—even sharing the bill with Alex Chilton at CBGB in New York. Kurtz was surprised that Omnivore was interested in putting out the Three Hits' five track record for RSD in 2013. His reaction:

> "In my mind, Hib-Tone provided the template for what I thought RSD releases should be artist-driven, limited, handmade, sold only by the band and in record stores, etc. That music is from a long time ago. I told [Omnivore] just tell me that you're still going to speak to me when they don't sell because I know what we're up against. But yeah, I was thrilled to have it happen. Omnivore did a fantastic job on the package."

And much to Kurtz's surprise, the one thousand copies of the Three Hits record ended up selling out.

Sundazed/Modern Harmonic finds RSD's delicate balance

Founded by vinyl revival pioneer Bob Irwin, Sundazed Music and its more esoteric imprint Modern Harmonic has been very active in Record Store Day. "It's a very delicate balance trying to not over or under produce for many reasons," explains Jay Millar, who runs the labels' Nashville office. His birthday fell on the first RSD in 2008.

"We always try to nail the quantity where the fans get what they want and there's maybe one left for the person who shows up the next day. The last thing we ever like to see is our stuff still sitting in a store long after Record Store Day; thankfully it doesn't happen often with us. No one wants to leave a store with excess [inventory]. It's a tough call. We also don't want to underproduce and disappoint folks who wanted [particular records]. It's amazing how much thought goes into all of it, not just production numbers. These days, whether consciously or subconsciously, every title gets assessed as to whether or not it is a RSD title or not."

How Sundazed makes that determination is "a tough question," Millar admits.

"It's sort of a feel thing. The release certainly has to be special, I think timing is a big thing…can we wait until then, should we just do it now? Ultimately, it's up for RSD to vote on the titles, but we've pretty much vetted them before we submit; our batting average with them is pretty good. I'm writing this in March 2021. We already have some of our Record Store Day Black Friday projects in production. It's really shifted how we schedule things in part because it's so date sensitive, but there's also a logjam at the pressing plants the closer you get to the events."

Millar is in a good position to comment on pressing matters because until a few years ago he was director of marketing from 2007 through 2015 for United Record Pressing, the largest US plant. The impact of RSD on URP's business was "tremendous," Millar reports, "Not just impacting the buildup to the date, but it helped expand the public consciousness of 'vinyl wish.' I'm sure RSD created new vinyl fans that became record store regulars. Over time, as RSD grew and with the additions of RSD Black Friday, they grew so much that it was just like our calendars shifted to two seasons, RSD and Black Friday. It was pretty much the day after one of them that we'd start taking [URP] orders for the next because there was always a logjam of people trying to join in on the fun."

Resonance makes RSD vinyl economics work

What makes the jazz label Resonance's archival vinyl releases very unique is that they're only available on Record Store Day and the titles usually sell out on the day itself, making them extremely coveted in the after-market. Resonance's first RSD release in 2012 was a ten-inch LP of Bill Evans in translucent cobalt blue: selections from Live at Art D'Lugoff's *Top of the Gate*.

"Initially, at first, we just put out ten-inch records for RSD with selections from the forthcoming albums to pique people's interest," explains Feldman, who previously worked at PolyGram and Rhino. "Then later we realized that we should just be putting out the whole albums for RSD itself, and it quickly became a vital element of our success. We could make the numbers work and ship sold out. That gave us the confidence to keep going."

"RSD has become a jazz destination, and it allows for the types of projects that we do to come out," explains Resonance copresident Zev Feldman. "It's hard enough to convince people to embrace projects like this and make the numbers work, so RSD provides the perfect vehicle for us at Resonance through these exclusive RSD releases. We're not greedy; we just want to make the economics of the project work so we can keep doing what we're doing," says Feldman.

In 2020, Resonance released live sets of Monty Alexander, Bill Evans, and Sonny Rollins, as well as unreleased sessions from Bob James. For jazz lovers who miss out snaring Resonance vinyl picks on RSD, a consolation prize is that they could get the music on CD. Only 6,000 copies worldwide of the three-LP Rollins Dutch collection were made. (The author thankfully managed to buy a copy online at Newbury Comics online, two days after being shut out on RSD Black Friday at three Manhattan brick-and-mortar stores.)

However, from the label perspective, figuring out the right vinyl quantity for such a limited edition isn't an easy task. "It frustrates me when folks can't get something, but truth be told, I think I was more conservative in the past," Feldman admits. "Over time, I've realized that I can go a little higher. I want people to be able to get the records, but I also want to make sure we're shipping sold out so we're not sitting on product in the warehouse. We're always trying to make sure we can set just the right number based on the actual anticipated demand."

Resonance takes extra lengths to create a deluxe package worth the higher price, points out Feldman.

"I think the typical jazz consumer is very discriminating, very educated. I've been able to put together elaborate packages and build dream releases. In our packages, I'm able to include as many relevant voices as I can find, whether they were in the actual band, they heard music when it was played or were close to the artists and their music in some way. I also see what we do as investigative journalism. At Resonance, as long as I can present a clear plan, my boss and copresident George Klabin is amenable to what I want to do within reason. We can't do everything every time, but I think we create more editorial content than most labels. If there's something a jazz consumer wants, they'll go to great lengths to get it. With the productions I'm involved with, it's like [the movie] *Field of Dreams*: If you build it, they will come. We really go above and beyond with editorial and packaging, elevating the art of record making. If people are going to be camping out and waiting in long lines, I want them to know that at the end of the tunnel awaits an amazing experience that they will treasure, something we worked really hard on. These projects are built to be collectible and coveted. Otherwise, we wouldn't do it this way. After all, they're all hand-numbered limited editions. Like a painting. The way I look at it, we're happy to have found a formula to make these projects work. RSD has allowed us to connect with so many consumers in the marketplace. It's not a money grab for us. We're not greedy. Like I've said before, we simply want to make the economics of each project work."

Feldman attributes Resonance's success largely to Record Store Day.

"I thought it was an exciting way to mobilize record buying globally and to celebrate brick-and-mortar retail. Such a big part of my life, education, and passion has been cultivated from the countless hours I've spent going to record stores. My love for record stores hasn't diminished one iota to this day, and record stores as guardians and purveyors of our culture are something I hold near and dear."

On Record Store Day, Zev usually leaves non-Resonance RSD titles for other consumers to snatch up for their collections. "I do sometimes buy records on RSD, but generally I kind of want to stay out of people's way on that day, to be honest. I'm in record stores constantly throughout the year, so every day is Record Store Day for me. On the actual day itself I'm usually busy monitoring the various feedback that comes through on social media, emails, texts, and all other forms of communication. It's always an exciting time, that's for sure, and I always feel very much a part of the experience through all my interactions with people."

RSD's "critical role" for ORG Music

Like Resonance, jazz figures prominently in the eclectic ORG Music, which in 2011 began amassing a rich reissue catalog including albums from John Coltrane, Miles Davis, Billie Holiday, and Thelonious Monk, in addition to alternative favorites Nirvana, Sonic Youth, and Bad Brains, among others. ORG was founded as Original Recordings Group by former Warner executive Jeff Bowers, who worked with Michael Kurtz to get Record Store Day off the ground in its early days.

RSD has been a lifeline for many independent record stores over the past decade, points out ORG general manager and partner Andrew Rossiter, who took over from in Music, who took over from Bowers when he was twenty-four years old. "It's hard to imagine what the landscape of music retail would look like without Record Store Day's growth, but I'm certain that it wouldn't be a pretty sight," adds Rossiter, estimating the label has released ninety individual RSD titles to date, including Black Friday releases.

"As a vinyl-focused independent label that relies on indie stores for the majority of our sales, Record Store Day has played a critical role in our own growth and success. With ninety RSD (and RSD Black Friday) releases under our belt, and more scheduled for this year (2021), I expect that RSD will continue to be crucial to our business."

Other Music and Secretly Canadian

Outlasting the massive Tower Records across the street for a decade, Other Music, a small downtown Manhattan record store succumbed to market forces, underscoring what record stores can be up against. By the time it closed, its rent was twice as much as when it started and sales were half of the store's peak.

"We were part of Record Store Day from the beginning," says Josh Madell, now head of label relations at Secretly Distribution, which handles the vinyl needs of seventy-five indie labels, "and we fully embraced it." The Secretly physical sales team works closely with its labels to develop, pitch, and manufacture RSD projects. "It's a year-round thing for us, and obviously that's Record Store Day's mission, making sure indie retail can stay relevant. In that respect, RSD is such a natural fit for us."

OFFICIAL SEAL OF
AMBASSADOR
2015
2015
DAVE GROHL
RECORD STORE DAY

I FOUND MY CALLING IN the back bin of a dark, dusty record store.

1975's K-tel's Blockbuster 20 Original Hits by the Original Stars featuring Alice Cooper, War, Kool and the Gang, Average White Band and many more, bought at a small record shop in my suburban Virginia neighborhood; it was this record that changed my life and made me want to become a musician. The second that I heard Edgar Winter's "Frankenstein" kick in, I was hooked. My life was changed forever. This was the first day of the rest of my life.

Growing up in Springfield, Virginia, in the seventies and eighties, my local independent record stores were magical, mysterious places that I spent all of my spare time (and money) in, finding what was to eventually become the soundtrack of my life. Every weekend I couldn't wait to take my hard earned, lawn mowing cash down for an afternoon full of discovery. And the chase was always as good as the catch! I spent hours flipping through every stack, examining the artwork on every cover, the titles and credits, searching for music that would inspire me, or understand me, or just to help me escape. These places became my churches, my libraries, my schools. They felt like home. And I don't know where I would be today without them.

More recently, I've been fortunate enough to have the opportunity to rediscover this sense of excitement, that magical feeling of finding something all one's own, by watching my kids go through it. Let me tell you: Nothing makes me prouder than watching my daughters spin that first Roky Erickson LP one of them picked out for their very own on one of our weekend trips to the record store. Or to watch the reverence they have as they handle their Beatles vinyl. How carefully they replace the albums into their sleeves, making sure they're placed back onto the self in the proper sequence. Watching them realize how crucial and intertwined every part of this experience is, I relive the magic of my earliest experiences with vinyl singles and albums, their artwork, liner notes etc. all over again and again.

I believe that the power of the record store to inspire is still alive and well, and that their importance to our next generation of musicians is crucial. Take an afternoon (and some hard-earned lawn mowing money) and please support them.

You never know, it might change your life forever, too.

—Dave Grohl, 2015 Record Store Day Ambassador

CHAPTER NINE

Gimme More

*Artifact: "an object made by a human being,
typically an item of cultural or historical interest."*

*[Everything from a Flaming Lips record that is infused with the blood
of its guest stars to a mini-record player, Record Store Day never fails
to deliver the unusual.]*

ON THE SECOND RECORD STORE Day in 2009, Nashville record
store Grimey's learned how the festivities could go awry. The Avett
Brothers were scheduled to hit the stage at 1:00 p.m. and the folk-
rock band drew a much bigger crowd than anticipated. "Attempting
to get a better view of the band, fans climbed and broke the fence
along one side of the parking lot," Doyle Davis remembers. "I was
losing my mind, thinking somebody's gonna die."

That scary moment during the Avett Brothers set was
immortalized on the cover of an RSD seven-inch record, points out
Anna Lundy, Grimey's head buyer, manager, and event coordinator
since 2004.

> "The picture shows just an ocean of people. The photograph
> was taken while the Avett Brothers were playing from the
> balcony on this old building, overlooking the parking lot.
> It was wild. There were so many people watching from
> the [building's other] balconies that I started freaking out,

'Oh, my God, are the balconies going to hold these people?'
And I just remember walking all the way up to the top of
the stairs, where there weren't supposed to be people, and
trying to get them to move. I lost my voice by that point.
There were almost as many people that came to see the last
band of the day, Mutemath, when it was dark, bookending
this crazy day."

Luckily no one was hurt and it didn't prevent other national acts
playing sets at Grimey's on RSD, including Jason Isbell and Paramore.
The Grimey's event was a metaphor for what was happening with
Record Store Day. The event was clearly growing bigger and bigger,
and it was time to make some additions. By 2010, the clamor
to create a second Record Store Day to handle more events and
releases sometime later in the year became too loud to ignore.
The answer was to upend the corporate marketing event known
as Black Friday (with its cheap DVD players and microwaves) and
turn it into another excuse to throw a party at a record store with
special Record Store Day releases and events. For the inaugural
launch, Record Store Day once again partnered with Metallica to
release the bands live performance captured in the basement of the
Nashville record store Grimey's on June 12, 2009, just two months
after the band had launched Record Store Day itself. Kurtz explains,
"We talked to Q Prime, Metallica's management, about once again
changing the game by doing a massive record store event around
Black Friday and they said yes, and gave us another huge gift. U2 was
also generous and gave their full support with another unique vinyl
EP made specifically for participating Record Store Day stores called
Wide Awake in Europe. Together these two records, along with
offerings from George Harrison, Bruce Springsteen, Soundgarden,
Killing Joke, Tom Petty and the Heartbreakers, Grinderman, Black
Keys, The Doors, Roky Erickson & the Black Angels and about twenty
other releases, launched Record Store Day's first Black Friday."

Because the magical events that occur at record stores on the big day are often local, and unknown outside of a region, it is the unique, limited-edition records that so many music fans focus on. So how does something like the Metallica and U2 Record Store Day releases come about? Kurtz explains:

> "I run the proposed Record Store Day release by a bunch of key record store owners who have been in the business on average for forty years. We just go over what makes sense? Does it make sense for a Record Store Day release? Is it unique enough? Is there something special about it? Is it already widely available?"

RSD receives submission pitches from labels, distributors, artists, and managers. An RSD committee throughout the year sifts through about one thousand LP, EP, and 45 proposals for reissues and never-before-released fare, of which usually half are approved. Kurtz gives feedback why things may have not been selected, estimating about a quarter of what's pitched is rejected. In recent years, the list—including Black Friday—usually numbers about 500 worthy titles that pass the committee's muster. RSD records are pressed in finite quantities, and most are not to be repressed in the future despite demand. The most memorable releases set a bar for creativity not only for the music itself, but also packaging or the vinyl itself. Ho-hum is not going to cut it for music fans. Sometimes they're gimmicky or outrageous.

For example, for RSD 2012, ten copies of the seven-inch bonus single of *The Flaming Lips and Heady Fwends* had its vinyl infused within the actual blood of chief Lip Wayne Coyne, as well his record guests Bon Iver, Yoko Ono, Ke$ha, and Chris Martin. Yes, their actual blood. The RSD album had a run of 10,000 copies. After RSD, Coyne later made ten copies of the blood-infused LP and sold them each for $2,500 for charity.

The Flaming Lips repeated the liquid record with beer in one hundred copies of a seven-inch single for "The Story Of Yum Yum and Dragon" and "Beer in Your Ear." But Wayne & Co. went one step further by enlisting perennial RSD sponsor Dogfish Head Alehouse to create an actual new beer brand, "Dragons & Yum Yums" (hence, the two related songs) and official beer of RSD 2018. For the occasion, the band released 5,600 copies (only 100 with beer) of the single in pink vinyl single featuring two new songs. (See the list below for other unusual Flaming Lips RSD releases.)

Liquid-filled records are difficult to ship, Third Man Records head Ben Blackwell knows from experience, but that didn't stop TMR from putting out in 2012 on RSD a blue-liquid filled twelve-inch record of Jack White's "Sixteen Salteens"/"Love Is Blindness." (Like Wayne Coyne, Jack also often outdoes himself on RSD, to wit his "Fastest Record Made," see Chapter Ten.) Only 500 copies of Third Man's liquid-filled record that was manufactured by United Record Pressing were available in Third Man Records' Nashville store, explains Blackwell, who cites a prototype Disney record that was liquid filled. "I think Disney made one and it never went anywhere, so [TMR's] is the first commercially released liquid-filled record," he adds.

It's important to note that Record Store Day itself doesn't manufacture or ship records as RSD is not set up for either task, and many of the crazy designs and packages demand special shipping and expertise. Here are some of RSD's more unusual and fun vinyl offerings:

- Geographically shaped picture discs, such as in 2013 Toto's *Africa,* containing the band's biggest hit "Rosanna," backed with "Africa," die-cut with the continent.

- Not to be outdone by Twenty-One Pilots, their RSD 2015 record was shaped as the state of Ohio, where they formed in 2009.

- Sir Paul on RSD 2015 reportedly snuck into stores only one hundred copies of a top-secret twelve-inch single "Hope for the Future" (Sweet Thrash Mix). Only one hundred copies were shipped to stores, which were instructed to: 1) not tell anyone; 2) not include that single record it received with the RSD releases but rather the "McCartney" section; and 3) price it at $9.99. Rumor has it that Macca himself hand-initialed some of the copies on the plain white label.

- Foo Fighters' RSD 2021 LP *Hail Satin* consisted of cover versions of the Bee Gees and a live side, combining for a completely unique album to support record stores.

- No two 12-inch singles of the 1,000-record run were alike for the Liars' 2014 RSD release of "Mess With a Mission," which embedded differently configured and colored strings within the clear vinyl of each disc.

- Similarly, Jack White's Third Man Records for 2011 RSD pressed peach-colored rose petals into the clear vinyl of Karen Elson's seven-inch single "Vicious," a Lou Reed cover version that contains the opening line, "She hit me with a flower."

- Wu-Tang Clan's Ol' Dirty Bastard for RSD 2016 released a die-cut of his faux public assistance card (originally displayed on his solo debut LP, *Return To The 36 Chambers*) that played "Brooklyn Zoo" and "Shimmy Shimmy Ya" on the A & B sides.

- While we're on hip-hop, let's not forget Slick Rick bundling for RSD 2017 a sixteen-page children's book titled "Children's Story" with the reissue of his LP *The Great Adventures of Slick Rick*. The book, complete with wipeable puffy pages, tells the story of the little boy who misled police.

- Switching to country music-related printed matter—a coloring book/graphic novel—also figured in the Buck Owens RSD 2012 Flexidisc, containing four of the musician's greatest hits. Originally published in 1970, the publication tells his story to stardom.

- Doors drummer John Densmore's book *Unhinged* became an official 2013 Record Store Day book and RSD also arranged a tie-in tour of record store appearances. Of course, The Doors' seemingly endless vault of unreleased material are annually among the most sought-after RSD releases. The most popular one included The Doors album curated by record store owners and put together by Doors' producer/engineer Bruce Botnick.

- Scent is another recurring gimmick, such as the marshmallow odor that emanated on RSD 2014 from the white vinyl of Ray Parker, Jr.'s "Ghostbusters" theme song from the 1980s movie classic.

- The venerable TV show *South Park* honored putrid character Mr. Hankey with a Christmas Classics RSD 2016 record laced with a chemical smell.

- For RSD 2015, Metallica harked back to the cassette format of their youth to replicate its 1982 seven-song demo, faithfully printing the J-card of handwriting of the then eighteen-year-old Lars Ulrich's tracklist. RSD 2017 also featured notable cassettes from Sublime and Paul McCartney.

- Beastie Boys' "Sabotage" 3" record, with original album artwork celebrating its twenty-fifth anniversary.

- Childish Gambino "because the internet," with a seventy-two-page screenplay.

- Frank Kozik designed 6" tall vinyl Nick Cave figure.

- David Bowie was a big supporter of Record Store Day during his lifetime. For example, a ten-inch RSD 2014 Black Friday release previewed two songs "'Tis a Pity She Was a Whore" and "Sue (Or In A Season Of Crime)" from what turned out to be his swan song LP, *Blackstar*, released two days before his death on January 8, 2016. Since then, multiple singles and live albums have been released for RSD.

As previously noted, Wayne Coyne fully grasps the idea of creating something special for Record Store Day, and he repeatedly outdoes himself. For RSD 2013, the Flaming Lips created only twenty copies of a plastic package in the shape of a frog, which contained a cassette of the band's 1983 demo recording. In addition, when the frog's mouth opened, the song played from a built-in device featuring a pitch-change capability.

CHAPTER TEN

Born to Run

"Half of [the customers] weren't really coming for the Record Store Day titles as much as just wanting to be a part of the event...."
—Jim Henderson, Amoeba Records

[Record stores Amoeba, Music Millennium, Grimey's, Waterloo, Brittany's, and Guestroom echo how RSD year after year sets sales records.]

RECORD STORE DAY CONTINUED TO build to the point that in 2013 Michael Kurtz received a phone call informing him that the French government was bestowing the honor of "Chavalie De L'Ordre Des Arts Et Lettres" and asked if he could fly to Cannes, France, to make his acceptance speech in French.

> "I was pretty scared to accept as I knew that William S. Burroughs, Phillip Glass, and some other exceptional people had been bestowed this French version of Knighthood. I also knew I'd never be able to master the language well enough to deliver a speech in French. Plus, it was a bit awkward as I didn't like the idea of being perceived as taking sole credit for Record Store Day. I felt more comfortable when I arrived. Fleur Pellerin, the French Minister of Culture, called me a genius for what I had accomplished with Record Store Day, as it empowered local businesses in a way that hadn't been done before. I was comfortable with that characterization as Record Store Day is a community event. It was an exciting

time and my acceptance speech was largely about the love we'd received from artists and the amazing community of record stores around the world that made it all possible."

It is these record stores that are often in the artists' mind when they create their music or decide how they want it released into the world. The stores are a microcosm of life and art. To really understand the impact of these stores and Record Store Day you have to hear it from record store owners themselves.

Music Millennium of Portland, Oregon

If you ask Terry Currier, who started working in record stores in 1972 and has 100-percent owned Portland's Music Millennium since 1996, "One way or another Record Store Day wouldn't happen without me." What he means by that audacious statement is that his stand against the major label distributors trying to strong-arm indie record stores from selling used CDs led to them initially banding together, soon to form CIMS, in which he became its first vice president and the two other RSD coalitions that followed.

When country singer Garth Brooks held a press conference in 1993 where he said he didn't want his new album sold in stores that sold used CDs, Currier held a protest barbeque in the back parking lot of his store, encouraging Portland residents to burn their Brooks CDs, records, and tapes. A hundred people showed up, and so did local TV and radio stations and newspapers; the national media picked up the story.

Currier's crusade began earlier that year when the then six major labels attempted implementing a uniform policy that prohibited stores from selling used CDs if they wanted marketing or advertising money. "At the time, used CDs were only about five percent of my business, but it was the principle of the whole thing that they were trying to tell me what I could do in my store," explains Currier, who sent his objections in a three-page letter to about 125 top label and distribution executives, and all the trade publications, which started covering "this little war between me and the industry."

Currier won support from other independent stores, who wanted to know if there was anything they could do to help. "We pulled all our stock of all Garth Brooks product in the store within the next ten minutes. I bought an ad in the next Wednesday's newspaper, inviting the public to come down to our store that next Friday and we would barbecue the Garth Brooks CDs, posters, VHS tapes, and records out in the back parking lot." Currier printed for his staff chef hats and aprons that said, "Barbecue for Retail Freedom."

This happened pre-internet, and even without social media, it was apparent from the press coverage that Currier's crusade was getting attention. Six months went by and nobody was conceding anything. Mark Cope of the Album Network called me about the Garth Brooks press conference. So he decided to take a West Coast road trip with an employee from Canada to Mexico, stopping along the way to hold similar barbecues at nine record stores along the way with coverage from *The New York Times, Rolling Stone,* CNN, the Country Music Channel, and *Forbes* magazine. When the road trip hit Berkeley at Amoeba Records, the campaign hit the five o'clock news. That night Currier and his road trip companion Fred wore their barbecue t-shirts to the San Francisco Giants baseball game. "People were yelling at us the whole night, 'there are the barbecue guys.'"

Currier then managed to schedule meetings in Los Angeles with all the heads of distributors. A record store on the east coast already filed a class-action suit against them over the issue. Currier was hoping they could avoid having lawyers involved. "Just several weeks later four majors rescinded their policies, and we beat them," he says, realizing that his efforts paid off. The icing on the cake for Currier was Brooks eventually saying on national TV when asked about the ruckus that started in Portland, "I think people should stand up for what they believe in." And you still won't find any Garth Brooks products in Music Millennium.

But more importantly for Currier, the protest's lasting dividend was independent stores—which up to that point hadn't shared trade secrets—recognized their collective power, an early precursor to what led to RSD. Indie stores began adopting new artists, and helped make a difference on the sales charts, he points out. That sharing of information led to the creation of the aforementioned Coalition of Independent Music Stores (CIMS) and the two other coalitions: the Music Monitor Network, which turned into the Department of Record Stores (DORS), and Alliance of Independent Music Stores (AIMS).

"Then in 2007, the three coalitions got together and put together Record Store Day, so I guess if we want to go back we can thank Garth Brooks for Record Store Day," Currier laughs. "Without Record Store Day, I don't know where record stores would be today," Currier says. "We really embraced Record Store Day and that first one was so great for us, and the second RSD was even better."

Waterloo Records of Austin, Texas

Even though Terry Currier is in Portland, Oregon, and John Kunz is in Austin, Texas, it turns out they're best friends, a fact I didn't learn until my call with Kunz. They both pushed for the formation of CIMS and saw the value in Record Store Day.

Locally, Kunz, owner of Waterloo Records, enlisted back in 2008 the dozen or so record stores in Austin. "I went to all of them and said, 'Hey, we're going to be doing this thing in April. Everybody should sign up with Record Store Day and get involved. This is a great way for us to give a big group hug to the Austin music community.'"

For the first RSD, Kunz received 100 percent participation from what was essentially Waterloo's competition. While some of the stores went out of business, others in recent years started up and there are a few less than what operated fifteen years ago. Every year, the shops pool their resources to take a full-page advertisement in the *Austin Chronicle* the week before RSD or Black Friday activities, including the three drops of 2020 and two drops of 2021, promoting the "Austin RSD Crawl." Divided equally, each store gets the same space with their listing. The ad more recently took into account the pandemic of 2020 and 2021 by noting stores that were offering online, limited in-store sales, or curbside delivery of orders.

Unlike the RSD Crawl that Warner Music Group began in 2016 that involved fans buying a sixty-five-dollar ticket and hopping on a bus that went store to store at set times, Austin participants needed to figure out their own transportation and hit the stores at their pace. "Yeah, they stole my name," Kunz says drolly. The Austin stores all agree to give local crawl fans discounts on regularly priced merchandise (but not RSD releases) if a sales receipt can be produced from one of the other stores. "There was a time at the very beginning of Record Store Day when so many stores were saying it was the biggest sales day in the history of their store," Kunz comments. As far as Waterloo is concerned, its biggest sales day then was typically December 23, however by 2013 or so, RSD consistently took in more money. "All of a sudden, Record Store Day was my biggest day of the year," he remembers.

Managing RSD in-store artist appearances, while making sure people had enough time to buy the special releases, became a crowd-control challenge if not headache for Waterloo, Kunz explains.

"We finally had to say we can no longer hold store performances on Record Store Day. We had to tell them, 'Sorry, we're at capacity. The band's going to be signing for an hour.' You don't want to be in the situation of telling somebody 'I'm sorry, we're at capacity. You can't come in.' The problem arises when the customer is already in the store and knows the band is scheduled to play in forty-five minutes. No one's gonna leave…they're gonna stay to get their record autographed. [They realize if they] come back in two hours, they might not be able to get it. That's just not the message you want to give somebody after you've put in so much promotional effort into getting them to come to the store that day. For a lot of people, [Record Store Day] was their reintroduction to record stores, or in some cases, their introduction entirely. There's a whole generation of kids that didn't have any need for a record store because they were burning CDs or downloading, and now they're streaming. They've got all the music they want for ten bucks a month or watching ads [on YouTube] on their phones. So it really is an art and culture community that we've created. It's an incredible glue for all of us music-loving freaks."

Currently, vinyl takes up more than half of Waterloo's floor space and 85 percent of the sales and evolved since 2008 steadily away from CD that he attributes to RSD for creating enthusiasm for the format.

Vintage Vinyl of Fords, New Jersey

Rob Roth, the owner of Vintage Vinyl in Fords, New Jersey, was sitting in his favorite NYC restaurant with Michael Kurtz. It was 2007. Rob had known Michael as the man who ran the Music Monitor Network, a coalition of independent record stores. At that time, Rob was actually a member of a *rival* coalition, but that didn't matter. Rob thought Michael an affable man as they'd been acquainted for years, often attending the same music-related conferences and concerts. As record store owner, Rob is a pragmatist and considered Michael a dreamer. Rob thought the world needs dreamers to get the big things done and that the idea that Michael was about to present was huge.

The business of record stores had recently taken a bad turn… cratering, based on media coverage and public perception of all the big names in record retailing—the national chain stores—had closed, or were in the process of going away forever. Seemingly overnight, the Compact Disc, which had brought huge profits to the record business for years, was quickly becoming irrelevant.

A kid in his college dorm room in 1999 launched Napster, a digital file-sharing program that was FREE! One CD uploaded and shared became the master for an infinite amount of free copies. It's hard to sell something that is available for free elsewhere. As the music industry fought Napster, Apple had embraced digital technology and launched a paid download site called iTunes, where access to individual songs was even more convenient. Labels grudgingly licensed its music to Apple, which sold each song for 99 cents and complete albums for $9.99

However, Rob saw a niche vinyl market developing among hipsters and LP fetishists. Vinyl, which had been written off by those in power at the major labels, was starting to be a format that many customers wanted. Maybe it was because they were not readily available, or maybe it was something else?

Rob thought that those who grew up with vinyl records found that they preferred the sound of LPs over the digital format. It was warmer, and more "natural," when played through the right equipment. The 12"x12" artwork could be enjoyed in its original expansive canvas; after all, the music is only part of an album presentation. For others, it's the whole ritual of taking the record out of the sleeve, placing it on the turntable, cleaning the disc, dropping the needle and then hearing it lock into the groove. There is magic there!

Rob noticed that teenagers and college-aged kids seemed fascinated with the format. It was not from their parents' generation, but from their grandparents'! He saw that they embraced vinyl as a way to rebel against the status quo. They were coming into the time of their lives when music defines their very existence, and they are once again known by their listening habits. The record store, then, is where you go not just to buy music, but to be among your community. (Some customers met their spouses in his store; some took their engagement or even their wedding pictures on his stage!) It's where you go to see what others are buying, to ask the clerks what *they* are liking, what's selling, what's playing on the store stereo? "Hey, that's great, I never heard that band before. Do you have it in stock?"

Rob thought that the big idea Michael presented that day at lunch was a way to capture this energy: a Record Store Day with every independent record store in the country celebrating vinyl records and the record stores themselves, serving as music cathedrals and music lovers their congregants. What did he think of it? He thought it would be wonderful if it could happen but didn't see a path for it to succeed. There were so many obstacles to hurdle. For one, vinyl manufacturing had virtually ceased. Very few pressing plants were left in the US. Not only were the machines that press records scarce, so were the people that knew how to cut masters, and other very specific skills required for creating a finished vinyl product.

Record company executives had to be convinced that there was a market to sell vinyl records, and that there were profits to be made. In the mid- to late 1980s the Compact Disc exploded as a convenient vinyl alternative with superior sound. (The fact that it actually cost less to manufacture and the record companies could charge a lot more made it very appealing to the bean counters.) A few years earlier Rob had a meeting with the head of a major distribution company where he explained the small but growing interest in the LP. The distribution head said, "The only thing an LP is good for is to clean pot, now get out of here!"

Nonetheless, Rob believed in the appeal of records. The name of his store is Vintage Vinyl, and back in 1979 when he first opened his door, vinyl was the only music format he carried. For serious fans and collectors, it was the only way to listen. Tapes, whether eight-track or cassette, sounded inferior. Maybe you had some for the car, but to listen seriously, the LP was it.

In the nineties, some music collectors actually rebought their whole record collection on CD, selling their LPs, which they were convinced were not as good. But by 2008, many of them wished they had kept their vinyl collections.

"We finished our great meal, and I told Michael, "I don't know how you're going to accomplish this, but if you do, you'll have all my support." Ultimately, I believe it was the artists, not the suits, who made Record Store Day possible. The artists wanted to see and hear *their* music on long-playing full-size records—the same format on which their heroes released their work. Their support was a very important piece for this to be successful. A year or two later, as my staff and I prepared for the first Record Store Day, we scheduled six or seven touring bands to perform live on our in-store stage. The artists were way into this Record Store Day idea, and they weren't alone. The traditional press, radio, and TV were embracing it, too. National TV news positioned Record Store Day as a human-interest story. I got calls from radio and TV reporters who wanted to cover the event at my store. I think the *Wall Street Journal* even called me for a comment! And, most importantly, throngs of music fans came back to the store. It was a celebration! What made Record Store Day so brilliant—and the key to its success in my opinion—was that the records offered for sale that day were very desirable not only because of the great music, but because they were limited releases: Get 'em while you can, 'cause they won't be making any more. Before Record Store Day, some independent record store owners like myself had been looking at a fast slide into oblivion; we saw no future. Then, overnight, the clouds parted and the sun shined down. Each year, Record Store Day became our busiest day ever. If we had a slow winter, Record Store Day would come just in time to rescue us."

Amoeba of Hollywood, California

On June 27, 2007, Sir Paul McCartney took the stage of Amoeba Records in Hollywood, California, and less than a year later the first Record Store Day took root. "This has to be the most surreal gig ever. The management has asked me to point out no shoplifting please," the former Beatle said from the stage. After nearly 1,000 people sang

"Hey Jude" with him, it occurred to him this was no ordinary gig. "I'd like to take a moment to take this all in," Paul urged the audience to consume the specialness of what they and he just experienced.

Perhaps McCartney was transported back to 1961 Liverpool and the record department of NEMS (North End Music Stores), owned by the family of Brian Epstein. It's where Paul and his scruffy-looking bandmates would check out the latest American imports as potential song additions to their repertoire. Curiosity set in for Epstein, who kept on getting requests for a single "My Bonnie" that the nascent Beatles recorded in Germany uncredited and was getting played on local radio. Their soon-to-be manager then checked out their lunchtime performance at the nearby Cavern Club, and you know what happened next.

Sir Paul's sentimental memories of the importance of record stores to the Beatles, as well as culture in general, pays tribute to all the entrepreneurs who keep the faith in serving their customers with physical music. In this chapter, we highlight the grit and gumption of seven longtime store owners, who explain how Record Store Day gave a new lease on life to their and employees' livelihoods, and they've made each event special for their customers.

Amoeba co-owner Jim Henderson remembers the first year the three-store chain focused on selling discounted posters, DVDs, and other merchandise around RSD, as well as putting out extra bins of used vinyl on the Hollywood store's stage where bands played until the pandemic.

> "Those are traditions that we kept up, year after year. So when Record Store Day would come, we would always tie in;…it's one of our biggest sale days at the store, we could also get…discounts on a lot of other things…that Amoeba has to offer to kind of go along with the party vibe, you know, we just kind of rode that wave. And as years went on, we also introduced an outdoor scene. The past six or seven years [leading up to 2019], we would create a bit of a scene

outside on the street with tables of bargains, caricaturists and food and drink vendors, and make it a real celebration."

By that point, Amoeba introduced a "menu," containing the list of titles, which were circulated to customers. Henderson lays out the routine.

"People line up outside and just basically make their picks on the menu. We pick up the menu, we take it inside the store, fill the bags, and then bring the customers in to buy their stuff right up front. And then once they're done buying, they could leave their purchases, bag checked and head in and shop for other stuff. It really was born out of the idea of pushing, shoving, fighting, and overcrowding. Everybody going after that twelve-inch, or whatever was the big thing each year, and just kind of going no-holds-barred. We had people taking chunks and hiding them and then telling their friends where they put them. It just became something that far exceeded the fandom and kind of craziness than we expected. We took steps to make it a little bit more organized, a first-come, first-serve type of situation. Our customers always really responded favorably to it based on the amount of emails and comments and compliments we got about doing [RSD] the right way and keeping things simple and light-hearted so people can have fun with it rather than looking like they were going into a rugby stadium. When the doors opened, it kind of worked out. The San Francisco store adopted it in 2020 for Covid-19 protocols for the RSD Drops. And you know, they may consider keeping it, you know, as Record Store Day goes along because it took away some of the grief."

With each RSD year after year, Henderson remembers, "We kind of got busier and busier with more titles. Probably somewhere around the fifth or so year, the Record Store Day sales surpassed, or what would traditionally be our busiest day of the year, the Saturday before Christmas. With Record Store Day 2018, we far exceeded our Saturday-before-Christmas numbers. It became a thing that we had to prepare for a month like we did for Christmas."

Amoeba's co-owner points out that shoppers on Record Store Day buying merchandise other than the RSD titles drove the sales numbers.

"You can pretty clearly figure out if you have, you know, hypothetically 6,000 to 7,000 pieces of Record Store Day titles, you're going to sell eighty percent of those at X amount of dollars. We found that our community really wanted to support record stores. So half of them weren't really coming for the Record Store Day titles as much as just wanting to be a part of the event, and, you know, show their support to the store and independent retail. So it was, you know, kind of a best of both worlds for us that we would deal with a really intense morning of Record Store Day stuff, and then wind to an afternoon a feel-good, busy shopping day with DJs, and the sidewalk sales and everything else going on at the party."

Amoeba pretty much brings in almost everything on the RSD and Black Friday annual product lists. "We'd skipped maybe just a couple titles," Brad Schelden notes, adding that Jim's estimate of 6,000 to 7,000 units of total RSD product in its stores was fairly accurate. "If there are about four hundred and fifty titles, you're bringing in on average about fifteen pieces of things, although we'd prefer sixty or ninety."

Always a fun thing for customers at Amoeba during RSD is the chance to get special T-shirts, screen printed in the store. Proceeds from the shirt sales always support a local music charity. "Our customers wear their Record Store Day shirts for years and years as a point of pride," adds Henderson.

Guestroom Records of Louisville, Kentucky

Guestroom Records was founded in Norman, Oklahoma, in 2002 and was an early adopter of Record Store Day. Lisa Foster became a professor at the University of Oklahoma in 2005. "I moved from Austin, where I worked at Waterloo Records," she explains. "The very first thing you do when you move to a new place is you find your indie record store, and I found Guestroom. It was really well curated, super smart."

In 2008, Foster started dating Guestroom co-owner Travis Earl, and by the second RSD she started helping out at the store, in addition to her university teaching. Guestroom then opened a second store in Oklahoma City, but Foster was getting homesick for her native Louisville, Kentucky, where a popular store, Ear Ecstacy, went out of business in 2011.

"In 2013 at one of our trips home to visit my parents we stopped at different record stores. They were all really good, but none of them were doing exactly what we did. And I was like, 'Let's try this. Either the community will respond to us [or they won't]." Travis and Lisa moved to Louisville, and their partner stayed in Oklahoma to run those stores. When the new store opened, Foster realized "a long-standing love and a lot of grief" remained for Ear Ecstasy. "People loved that store. I loved that store. I shopped at it. There was a lot of healthy skepticism, 'Who are you? Why are you here?'"

Guestroom delivered a well-curated store and soon found their local community when they opened in October 2013. "I think that people feel like we're theirs too. Give them a record store experience they've never had, and then you've got customers for life," says Foster, who received a taste in Norman, Oklahoma, of how Record Store Day helped to cultivate their store community, who showed up the next month for Black Friday. "Yeah, people found us," and for their first RSD in 2014, local bands played Guestroom. "It was small, but it was really good. Watching the customer base expand to me is the biggest gift of Record Store Day as an institution. There's no doubt to me that Record Store Day has been so instrumental in expanding the potential customer base for stores."

Brittany's Record Shop of Cleveland, Ohio

Brittany Benton opened her Cleveland record store Brittany's on March 23, 2018, knowing that Record Store Day was a month away. As an African-American woman, Brittany plies her trade in two fields that are dominated by men: deejaying and owning a record store. No stranger to being an entrepreneur, Benton already operated two other stores, but her new shop she felt was in a better location and had a better chance of reflecting her tastes as a club disc jockey known as DJ Red-I, part of the act on the local scene known as "Two Turntables and a Conga," which, pre-Covid, had been a regular monthly gig at the downtown club Rebar and Touch Supper Club.

"Everything shut down [in March 2020]. I was working on a residency, mostly hip hop. I DJ all over the city." The time off gave Benton time to rethink how the record shop could be improved.

> "I wanted Brittany's to be an extension of me and the music I grew up on and what I love to spin [as a DJ]. I'm pretty free with the genres, as long as it's got a deep groove and a nice rhythm like a funky country album. I would DJ with stuff that I sampled from making beats and the music that inspired me when I was growing up. I specialize with a small boutique-style shop with black and adjacent music like rock acts. I still carry a lot of Elton John. I really love Bowie, Timberlake, and stuff like that. In Cleveland, there were over a half dozen independent shops, but they all kind of specialized in different forms of classic rock....They have a different approach. I come from a lifestyle where I DJ to put food in the fridge and keep the lights on."

The pandemic forced Benton and the clubs where she deejays an extended pause, sell some records online, and for her, figure out a better location, which turned out to be a new place further on Cleveland's east side, scheduled as of this writing to be open the first week of April 2021.

For RSD 2018, Brittany's managed to tie into promotions from local brewery Great Lakes and its "Vinyl Tap Beer," gear from Audio-Technica, and a vinyl fair, including two other stores. "So we had a huge day on that first Record Store Day," she remembers, noting that all three record stores get along really well. "It was definitely the goal to be open at least a month before Record Store Day [with the first Brittany's]. It might have been harder to get people's attention but the timing of Record Store Day definitely worked out. I figured it would be good to have the opening then to bring about awareness."

For the new store's opening in April 2021 with RSD being delayed until June 12, the community-minded Benton brought in other vendors to sell books and records (not just her stock), hoping that all customers who come by will find something they would like. "Since we're not having a Record Store Day in April [2021], I'm having the record and book fair on that Saturday. Since Covid-19, there haven't been any good book fairs last summer, because of Covid-19. I thought it'd be really good to bring people out."

As far as her own curation, Benton notes, "I said to myself that next time I open a shop, I want to really cater to that niche of people who's looking for a great hip-hop, reggae, soul record, just stuff like that."

The Groove of Nashville, Tennessee

Operating a record store is hard enough, but sometimes it could be a life-or-death situation for an owner. Jesse Cartwright, co-owner of The Groove, an RSD-participating store in Nashville, desperately needed a kidney transplant. Remarkably, his partner Michael Combs learned on December 31, 2019, that he was approved to be a donor match, which is extremely rare for a patient's non-relative.

In February 2019, Jesse started dialysis treatment at a clinic, for which he had to get up at 5:00 a.m. three days a week and get hooked up to a machine for "five or six hours and then go to work," explained Jesse on a December 2020 RSD podcast. He was diagnosed as a Type 1 Diabetic at sixteen years old, so by that point he had been dealing with a bad kidney for a quarter of a century. In 2017, the partners purchased The Groove, which in pre-Covid times was open seven days a week 11:00 a.m. to 8:00 p.m. Two years later, Jesse was looking at serious kidney failure. Jesse had an arm operation in May 2019 that allowed him to receive dialysis treatment via home, they kept the store going. But once Covid hit in March 2020, Jesse couldn't leave the house because his immune system was gone due to the kidney condition. He was hoping to hold out to also get a pancreas transplant at the same time he received Michael's kidney, but that wasn't meant to be. It was decided that both Cartright and Combs would have their operations on July 28, 2020.

Jesse's sister and a part-time employee kept The Groove going. An outpouring of support from customers shared stories of their loved one's going through dialysis or other heath ordeals. "Part of what kept me going is the store and our amazing customers," Jesse said.

Meanwhile, his mom was suffering from pancreatic cancer in Michigan, and she didn't have long. Jesse hadn't seen her in quite some time, and even though it was critical that he keep his regular doctor appointments to prevent rejection of Michael's kidney, they travelled to her and found a treatment center in Michigan. She passed away on September 11, 2020, but Jesse was grateful that he was able to share that time with her, as well as Michael's kidney that gave him literally a new lease on life. "We met sixteen years ago. I guess there was a reason why we were brought together."

Fingerprints of Long Beach, California

Besides RSD records featuring various gimmicky bells and whistles, or coveted band reunions, sometimes doing a good deed is the catalyst. Such was the case in 2017 with *Like a Drunk in a Midnight Choir*, Record Store Day's first album, a celebration of Leonard Cohen with contributing artists, including Glen Hansard, Joseph Arthur, Terry Reid, Mike Watt, and Donovan.

Record Store Day decided that it should be a philanthropic effort with proceeds from the record's sale going to the Pablove Foundation, which is dedicated to fighting pediatric cancer following the recent loss of Pablo, the six-year-old son of Jeff Castelaz, cofounder of the Los Angeles-based label Dangerbird Records and a former president of Elektra Records, and his wife, Jo Ann Thrailkill.

Among Pablove's fundraising efforts was a 1,300-mile bike ride led by Castelaz, who was supported by a group of doctors, engineers, entrepreneurs, and business executives. Since Jeff was in the business, it made sense for Record Store Day to also help in the most obvious context.

"We were looking for something that was music industry related without being music related," explains the record's executive producer Rand Foster, the owner of the Fingerprints record store in Long Beach. "Leonard Cohen had just died and somebody brought up the idea amongst that committee, we should go to Sony and [license] a greatest hits 'Record Store Day picks our favorite Leonard Cohen songs.'" Foster thought so many greatest hits collections of Leonard Cohen saturated that space. "I just felt like we could do something a lot more inspired."

Rand realized he could tap as talent many of the artists who played Fingerprints, and with whom he remained in touch and became friends. "At the time Glen Hansard posted on Facebook how devastated he was about Leonard's passing. Matt Costa had done the same. And Joe [Arthur] also did it, using their social media spaces to kind of grieve the loss of Leonard."

Kurtz suggested that Foster reach out to some of his record store's legendary connections, and within a week, he had a maybe from Dave Alvin—who ended up not being able to do it—but a yes from Matthew Ryan, a tentative yes from Hansard, and a yes from Arthur. "I think he was a little surprised that I was able to do that," remembers Foster, who suggested to Kurtz that others within the RSD family might want to get involved. "Michael thought other people might not have those kinds of connections to reach out and ask for this. So I was like, 'Okay, if you feel like I'm not stepping on toes, then you know, that would be awesome.' So I started making inquiries and kind of built it up from there."

The legendary folk singer Donovan ends the record with a live version of Cohen's "So Long, Marianne," the only live track on the album. How Foster reached the Scotsman showed his ingenuity. "A friend of mine helped him on some US projects, but he wasn't part of the team. He mentioned it to Donovan's manager, who said, 'He's gonna want to be involved in this.'"

The folk-rock statesman's participation proved somewhat challenging, despite being "absolutely delightful." After selecting the track and recording it at a concert in Denmark, Foster's production team were working on the track listing and artwork.

"He came back and said, 'I'm not okay with the name, you're going to have to change the name, you can't call it *Like a Drunk in a Midnight Choir* because that's disrespectful to Leonard'. And I said, 'It's really not'. We ended up spending probably an hour on the phone, talking about the thought behind it, and how it was celebratory and revelatory, and it was other people singing Leonard's songs. Ultimately, it came down to if it means Donovan can't be involved, that's going to be devastating in a whole lot of different ways, but I can't change the artwork or title.'"

Donovan called Foster the next day to say, "In my dreams last night, Leonard came to me from the 'Bardo,' and he likes your name," referring to the Tibetan Buddhism's state of existence between death and rebirth. Near disaster averted.

The participating musicians handled—and donated—the recordings of the album's dozen songs and production of the tracks; some were more elaborate than others. Hansard sent thirty-two tracks that had to be mixed down, while others came fully formed. In two or three instances, RSD covered their studio time, "but it was a couple of hundred bucks kind of thing," Foster explains.

When it was done, the *Like A Drunk in a Midnight Choir* album sold out and Foster had created the first RSD charity album, raising $10,000 for the Pablove Foundation.

Grimey's of Nashville, Tennessee

A few years ago, Concord's Donna Ross, who had recently relocated to Nashville at the time, had two work colleagues visit from Los Angeles: Craft Recordings president Sig Sigworth and senior vice president Mason Williams. They wanted to check out Grimey's, the iconic store. "So she just introduced me to [Sig] and we're just talking," recalls Grimey's co-owner Doyle Davis, who hosts a weekly radio show "Groovy Potential" on WXNA-FM. "I was just like, 'Man, I love what y'all are doing.' We talked about some of the releases, and I said, 'The "Jazz Dispensary" series, that's the shit! That's my stuff. When you put out one of those, somebody broke into my basement when I wasn't looking.'"

Launched in 2016, the "Jazz Dispensary" records feature overlooked, spaced-out jazz and funk tracks from the 1960s and 1970s from the Prestige label archives. The latest collections curated by co-owner, Doyle Davis and released on Record Store Day are adorned with equally mind-expanding cover design by Argentinian artist Mariano Peccinetti in an embossed sleeve.

A few months after the store visit, Davis received an email from Mason Williams at Craft, asking him "Hey, you want to compile one of these? All we can really offer is a $750 producer's fee. I hope that's okay." Davis was like, "I'll do it for free."

Record stores creating fun for their customers all over the world is at the center of Record Store Day. "Those of us on the inside definitely look at it that way," says Davis. Beyond Davis' work on the Jazz Dispensary, over the years, *Live at Grimey's* albums have featured such talents as Dawes, Cage the Elephant, Amos Lee, Justin Townes Earle, The Lone Bellow, Langhorne Slim, The Brummies, Kip Moore, and Metallica.

Good Records of Dallas, Texas

A diehard Alice Cooper fan when he was a teenager in the early 1970s, Michael Kurtz was ecstatic to learn from YouTube that four of the five surviving members of the original Alice Cooper band performed for its longest set since 1974 in Brazil at Good Records in Dallas, Texas, on October 6, 2015.

Two years earlier, the store's owner Chris Penn learned that Dennis Dunaway, the original band's bassist, was writing an autobiography, and he enquired about Dunaway doing a book signing/Q&A. After a year of persistence, Chris managed to get Dennis to agree. At Penn's urging, Dunaway then contacted guitarist Michael Bruce and drummer Neal Smith, and both were on board for the in-store and to play a few songs. Original guitarist Glen Buxton passed away in 1997.

It just so happened that singer Alice Cooper's solo band was opening on October 7 for Mötley Crüe, and the day before they had off. Knowing Cooper's penchant for golf, Penn then reached out to his management about Alice joining the Q&A portion. The stage was all set up with instruments and a professional sound and film crew to capture the impromptu, unrehearsed eight-song set for posterity. Two songs in, Alice lumbered onto the stage taking lead vocals over from Bruce. The last time they all shared a stage was in 2011 when they were inducted into the Rock 'n' Roll Hall of Fame.

Kurtz contacted Penn about putting out the performance on vinyl for Record Store Day. Cooper's lifelong manager shared the tapes with original Alice Cooper producer Bob Ezrin, who was so impressed with the audio quality and the unrehearsed performances that he mixed the tracks. Penn spared no expense for the packaging with the single and LP both getting a silver-foiled gatefold.

Only 2,700 copies of the live two-sided single ("I'm Eighteen" b/w "Is It My Body") were released for RSD Black Friday 2016, and the following year Alice Cooper's *Live From the Astroturf* was the best 45 package at the inaugural Making Vinyl about a year later. Then the full album, including eight greatest hits, was released on Black Friday 2018, and it won the best "Record Store Day" release at the 2019 Making Vinyl competition. The award was accepted by Dunaway and Bruce at the October 2019 Making Vinyl conference, who were also present for the screening, the Los Angeles premiere of the feature-length documentary.

The November 23, 2016, headline on the *Dallas Morning News* story about the single release says it all: "Be Thankful for Chris Penn and Alice Cooper This Record Store Day."

Easy Street of Seattle, Washington

On April 18, 2015, Seattle's Easy Street Records presented a special Record Store Day in-store performance by the legendary Northwest band, The Sonics, who had just released their first album in nearly forty years, *This Is The Sonics*. Tickets went on sale the day before the event, with all proceeds going toward funding Seattle radio station KEXP's move to larger headquarters at the Seattle Center.

The event was billed as "The Sonics (and Special Guests)," raising a great deal of speculation and excitement about the guests, who turned out to be a who's who of the local scene. At 10:00 p.m. with the store packed to capacity, the Sonics took the stage, and as night went on, they welcomed Pearl Jam's Eddie Vedder and Mike McCready, Chris Ballew

(Presidents of the USA), Ben Shepherd (Soundgarden), Van Conner & Mark Pickerel (Screaming Trees), original Sonics bassist Andy Parypa, Calvin Johnson (Beat Happening), Matt Lukin (Mudhoney), Emily Nokes (Tacocat), Bill "Kahuna" Henderson (Girl Trouble), and Rod Moody (Swallow). KEXP recorded and filmed the entire event, and the album *The Sonics Live At Easy Street* was released on vinyl the following year for RSD April 16, 2016. Speaking of Pearl Jam and Easy Street, the band did a surprise in-store performance at the store on April 29, 2005. An EP *Pearl Jam Live at Easy Street* was released on vinyl to celebrate Record Store Day on April 13, 2019.

Record Connection of Niles, Ohio

Whereas Metallica's involvement in RSD was initiated by Michael Kurtz, the Foo Fighters performing at Record Connection in Niles, Ohio, on RSD April 18, 2015, was leader Dave Grohl's idea. Grohl moved from Ohio with his family to Virginia when he was a young child.

Nearly five decades later, Grohl gets enlisted to induct Joan Jett into the Rock 'n' Roll Hall of Fame in Cleveland. He thought it would be fun to pay tribute to his roots. Record Connection, an hour away from Cleveland, was scoped out by an operative in Silva Artist Management (SAM), the firm that oversees the affairs of the Foo Fighters.

Situated in a nondescript strip shopping center, Record Connection has been owned and operated at this location by Jeff Burke since 1983. He bought it out of bankruptcy in 1980. The original store opened in 1973.

> "We almost went out of business shortly after I took over this place because eight-track tapes were discontinued, obsolete and nonreturnable, but my buddy didn't tell me that. So we were stuck with all those things. It just was a matter of marking them down to get rid of them. We never got out of records the whole time."

Record Connection has been involved in RSD since 2008.

"We've been big supporters. We throw a big party here every year. It's just not the records here. Bands play, coffee and donuts in the morning and legendary pizza parties and barbecued pork sandwiches and barbecued chicken. We put a large tent up, you know, in front of the store. Record Store Day merchandise is available inside and outside. So you know, we've been able to move the crowds around a little bit quicker."

That logistics knowledge will soon pay off big time. The surprise gig saga began with a phone call from California in late February 2015. "This gentleman introduced himself simply as 'JC.' His question to me was, 'Would you be interested in having a band play at your Record Store Day event?' I told him we always have a band, so yeah, we were very interested. We made some small talk back-and-forth. Then we got back to business. I ask, 'What band are you talking about?' And he says the Foo Fighters."

Burke knew Grohl was born one city over from Niles, where Dave's father and his uncles lived. In fact, his grandmother was a longtime bookkeeper for a local lumber company owned by one of Burke's best friends.

"I immediately replied, 'What do I have to do?' The Foo Fighters are hugely popular in this area. So he asks if I was a guy that he could trust? I told him, 'I'm Don Corleone. If you tell me something, I don't tell anybody. My ex-wife used to accuse me of being the perfect mafia guy because if somebody told me something, that's as far as it went.' So I told him I was trustworthy and wouldn't say a word. He said, 'Perfect, get the okays from my landlord. Contact the fire department, the local authorities,' all the people that would be instrumental. A few days after the call, somebody from New York faked me out. I can't remember his first name, but his last name was Rosenberg, a really nice guy with a backpack on. He said that he was traveling around the country, and his favorite thing to do was to stop in the local record stores and just see what they were all about, and check out their inventories and on and on and on. [He was] a kind of an animated guy, really easy to talk to."

A few days later, Burke receives a call from someone who works with Silva in California that they found an empty spot next to the store that he thought would work for the Foo Fighters event. A sewing store previously occupied the empty space that appeared ideal for a stage, and a separate area for a green room because it had a bathroom. Burke paid the rent on the space, as well as for eight policemen, and then the Foo Fighters hired eight more.

"They never, they never asked me for any additional money. Of course, I paid for refreshments, but I didn't have a whole lot of expense. They brought a stage crew in and a sound company from Cleveland. They gave us several hundred T-shirts that we sold for ten bucks apiece, and we gave all the money to charity. You know, they gave us some Foo Fighters posters, pens, stickers, some seven-inch singles that we were able to put in the Record Store Day tote bags."

Of course, Record Connection needed to stock up on Foo Fighters albums, and Silva and the Foo Fighters connected Burke with people at RCA and Sony to open a special account for him. "A vice president of sales took the order. I told him what I thought I would need. So he quadrupled everything. This was a credit arrangement, so we paid for whatever we sold, and they took back whatever we didn't sell. Win-win all the way around for my store."

Burke has no doubt that it all came about because Dave Grohl made it well known around his management's office that he wanted to play an independent record store for Record Store Day.

"Somebody planted the seed that right in Dave's [former] backyard there is an indie store that's been around for a long time. So I credit that guy really for putting the whole thing together. We just got it done, they wanted the room measured and pictures of the front and the back of the building and pictures of the breaker box. Anything they wanted done, we just jumped on it and did it. Nobody's gonna blow an opportunity like that. Mind you, I run the store by myself just like when I took it over. It's a tough business. Payroll can kill a little store like this. Another question John Cutcliffe asked me, 'Do you have adequate staff for this?' And I said, 'Oh, yeah, you know, we have adequate staff.' My dad, who was ninety-three at the time, volunteered to help and never missed a single RSD until last year when he was weak and unable to attend. My sister and her husband, two of my brothers, and several friends and some prior employees were the staff and continue to help each year. I suppose SAM figured it out, but they were pleased with our handling of the event. So little by little things developed, they put me in touch with a couple other people. Silva supplied specially produced promo products for the show like T-shirts and posters. They were so easy to work with. And, you know, anything they asked me to do, I just did it."

Burke needed to notify the police and fire departments what was being planned. They were very cooperative. "The police told us we were only allowed to have 150 in that room. And you know, the fire department told me that they could easily give us a permit for 200. But John Cutcliffe wanted it to be 150 because they were bringing their own people."

The Foo Fighters announced the Record Connection show on the Wednesday before Record Store Day, which Burke followed up with his own press release ten minutes later.

"The next day all this freight came in here. Two gigantic generators on a flatbed Caterpillar come rolling up to the front of my shop. They had a manifest in their hand and said, 'Yeah, we're supposed to deliver these things to your store.' And all I had to do was sign for it. And then all the equipment started showing up. I'm like, 'Man, this thing is going to happen.' It was almost like a dream."

The day of the gig mostly management people from Silva milled around with the road crew. *Rolling Stone* magazine sent a photographer and a writer.

"It was a beautiful day, about seventy-four degrees, which is kind of unusual in April for this area. It's normally a little bit chilly. It was a bright, sunny day. It couldn't have been better. I had to concentrate on keeping everything organized. We had a lot of things jumping around. We had to try to move the crowd around in this strip plaza. We didn't want everybody congregating around the store before it opened, creating a logjam with the parking and blocking people from coming to the other shops in the plaza. Dave rode in here on a motorcycle riding through the parking lot. I saw him ride by to the back of the plaza, where they had tents, food, and stuff."

Since they needed to get to Cleveland for the Rock 'n' Roll Hall of Fame show that night, there wasn't enough time to sign autographs for fans. The windows of the performance space were blacked out, so people not inside couldn't take pictures of the band.

"People could hear outside. I mean, it was plenty loud. I mean, it was pounding, just like a rock show. They were cranking you know, for one straight hour, one song into the other. It was just phenomenal. I didn't get to see Dave until after the one-hour show was done. A gal from the office took me back to see him and the band. They couldn't have been a nicer bunch of people. A local rental center donated some furniture, six recliners, and a refrigerator. I shook hands with Dave. He patted me on the back half a dozen times or so, thanking me for putting that together. And I'm thinking to myself, 'Man, I should be kissing your feet for what you did here,' but he gave me all the credit for everything."

Jeff ordered a welcome banner from Canada because he was afraid word would leak out about the Foo Fighters coming to town if he had done it locally.

"I couldn't breathe a word of this show. So if I would have had it done locally, somebody would spill the beans. So anyway, after the show, Dave told me, you know, he said the banner was a real nice touch. I told him the story about how we decided to get that banner done in Canada. He says, 'You're a regular fucking James Bond.' He got a big kick out of the story."

As a result of the Foo Fighters experience and Grohl's and SAM's endorsement of Record Connection, Jeff Burke managed to book Joe Walsh for an in-store. But the biggest bonus was the sales of Foo Fighters vinyl and CDs on Record Store Day.

"[The label] was very impressed by how much product I moved. It was hundreds and hundreds of albums, way more vinyl than CDs, a boatload of record albums and CDs. They even sent a rep from Sony who worked out of Chicago to oversee everything. So when I gave him the numbers, he said, 'Damn it, dude, you did good.' So it really paid off."

A year later, Burke went to see the Rolling Stones in San Diego, and was invited to the SAM office in Los Angeles, where he learned that another store in St. Louis was also considered for the Foo Fighters gig.

"When I was out in California, you know, I asked [Silva's] Kristen, 'I gotta get the real story from you because everybody's asking, how did this thing come about?' She told me the same story I gave you. After this Rosenberg fellow was here, they didn't go any further, they knew they could put it together here. For once in my life, I was in the right place at the right time. The stars aligned perfectly. We had a spot in this Plaza. Dave was from around here originally, is a Record Store Day ambassador, and he wants to play here before coming to Cleveland. I mean, it was just boom, boom, boom, boom, boom. Perfect alignment of the stars."

Gramaphone Records of Chicago, Illinois

Record store encounters often result in romances and sometimes marriages, but Chicago house music DJs Dani Deahl and Fei Tang *were married* in 2013 in a record store, Gramaphone in Chicago, where the DJs had their first date on RSD 2011. "We went to Molly's Cupcakes, picked up a dozen, and then headed over to legendary Gramaphone Records to dole them out and hang with the staff," Deahl wrote in The Vinyl District. She had booked Tang, who goes by the moniker "DJ Phives," for a dance party gig "so that he could ask me out on a date," which apparently went very well. "Fei told me later there was a specific moment when we were both crate digging, looked up and smiled at each other, and he resolved in his head that he would marry me… Little did I know Fei had already told friends that it was his intention to date me, even though we had never met."

Two years later, Gramaphone owner Jason Bradley gladly offered the premises, which crammed in more than fifty guests for them to tie the knot. Since neither were particularly religious, they both thought the store made sense for venue. Their wedding planner embraced the music theme by creating an invitation to look like a 45-rpm single and Ticketmaster stub.

In regard to the event's setting, Deahl told *Huffington Post*, "We weren't setting out to be weird or out of the box for the sake of doing it—we felt it was important to be genuine and thoughtful with all the details, so it truly reflected who we were as people." She is vice president for the Recording Academy Chicago chapter and is known for helming the YouTube series "The Future of Music." And when Tang is not spinning, since 2015, he's led "theIMAGED," a community organization of photographers and artists who create and plan charitable events.

Electric Fetus of Minneapolis, Minnesota

Prince tweeted on the morning of April 16, 2016, to remind everyone it was Record Store Day, and hinted he'd be at his favorite Minneapolis record store, Electric Fetus. About a half hour before the store closed, Prince showed up, buying six CDs, proving the event isn't only about limited-edition vinyl. Prince's selections:

1) Stevie Wonder, *Talking Book*

2) Chambers Brothers, *The Time Has Come*

3) Joni Mitchell, *Hejira*

4) Swan Silvertones, *Inspirational Gospel Classics*

5) Missing Persons, *The Best Of Missing Persons*

6) Santana, *Santana IV*

After making his purchases, Prince tweeted again: "FETUS, THANX 4 THE TUNES! ROCKED STEVIE'S TALKING BOOK ALL THE WAY HOME! #RecordStoreDay."

Prince died five days later.

Bull Moose Music of Portland, Maine

For RSD 2019, the metal band Mastodon released a limited ten-inch vinyl release of their cover version of Led Zeppelin's "Stairway to Heaven." Chris Brown recalls an ecounter at his Bull Moose location in Maine about thrity minutes after opening. "The store was really full. A woman came up to me and asked, 'Hey, can you help me get some stuff for my son?' So she took me over to this guy in a wheelchair. He had speakers mounted on either side of his head and wore a sleeveless denim vest with patches of all his favorite bands, such as Anthrax, like most metal guys I've ever met. He was super nice."

So Brown and the mom go through the list, and hit the bins, "turning into this big collaborative event involving the store's entire staff. 'Hey, does he want any seven inches?' someone asked. The Mastodon single was on the list. The person holding the last copy [in the store] decided that the guy [in the wheelchair] really should go home with the record. There was just this community spirit around this guy."

The wheelchaired metal fan's name was Mike Norton. He passed away in the summer of 2020. His mom Suzan Norton remembers the Mastodon single story vividly. "It just blew Mike away that the guy would do that. We knew what we were looking for. We're in the same section. The guy went to grab it. So I say to Mike, 'That's okay, we'll go to another Bull Moose,' and the guy says, 'No, you can just take this one.'"

Brown notes hanging out with Doors drummer John Densmore, who did a Bull Moose RSD in-store for his autobiography, was "pretty great because of the vibe he gives off the kind of person he is. But you know, that day with Mike [Norton] was more fun to me because it shows what Record Store Day has meant to music lovers."

Suzan and Mike loved going to all of Bull Moose's stores.

"I was twenty-four-seven caregiving for Michael because he could only use two fingers. That's all he could use. Anyhow, we've been going to Record Store Day since 2011 where they would always pick up the limited-edition posters, tote bags, and pins produced for each RSD. Music is really important to me too. I like a lot of bluegrass, Irish fiddle music. I'm a big Led Zeppelin head, and Pink Floyd. Those are my bands; also Aerosmith back in the day. Yeah, I love Record Store Day, as much as you. It was a blast, so much fun. Just go and just meet people, talk to people."

Mike's tastes ran to heavy metal, but he also liked old Hank Williams, and Mike and Suzan would go to concerts to see his favorite bands. Suzan says Mike always looked forward to celebrating Record Store Day.

"Motörhead was his favorite, then probably Slayer. We would go over the whole RSD list [in advance every year], and I would write down what he wanted. It was always a pretty lengthy list. Sometimes we'd get 45s. One time we got a Buck Owens comic book-type thing. We just got all kinds of stuff. Mike's room still is full of all of his vinyl and DVD collection. It was a lot of work to take him to different places, out of state because I had to make sure all his equipment and ventilator was charged. He had to breathe."

After taking care of Michael's medical needs all those years—she also had another son die young four years ago—Suzan recently started working at a hospital. She's also working on a film and book about her sons.

Third Man Records of Nashville, Tennessee

Also requiring perfect alignment without a second to spare was Jack White on RSD April 19, 2014, making the world's fastest record. In less than four hours, he recorded at Third Man Records' (TMR) Nashville headquarters' Blue Room straight to acetate two tracks in front of a live audience. White stepped onto stage at 10:00 a.m. and delivered with his band a forty-minute set from which "Lazaretto," the title of his then-forthcoming album set for release on June 10, on the single's A side and a cover version of Elvis Presley's "The Power of My Love" on the B side. The two acetates were then transported over for pressing and packaging to United Record Pressing (URP) 1.8 miles away. A photo from the packed performance was slapped on the seven-inch record's sleeves. Eight hundred copies of the seven-inch single were then delivered from URP and on sale at TMR within three hours and fifty-five minutes.

Easier said than done. Label chief Ben Blackwell, White's nephew, explains in detail how they were able to accomplish the feat and remembers project planning going back to late January or early February.

> "It was the most logistics we've ever had to consider in regards to an actual record release. And when I say logistics, we needed to specifically know, for example, how many records are going to be made per minute, and how are those records getting moved from the plant to the store? In any other situation of making a record it would be like 'We'll ship it FedEx, who cares? It'll get there in three days.' 'No, no, no. Who has the car? Who's driving these over?' There needs to be a solid answer because we're really hemming ourselves in with people's expectations. There were a handful of sit-down meetings between Third Man and URP all sitting in the same room, going over simple things like how does the lacquer get from Third Man to the pressing plant? We had to build out contingencies on every single level. Okay, if this goes wrong, where do we go from here? But it was fucking fun. It's almost like you never get to do something that crazy with that kind of pressure again."

"A potential hiccup occurred the evening before the soundcheck while testing levels for a test cut," explains Ben, who wasn't present for the mishap and glad he was asleep when it happened.

"It was a late night when we blew the cutter head. Blowing a cutter head is kind of like getting your transmission replaced. On a car it's not the end of the world, but you're not driving anywhere that day; professional help is needed, and it will take some time. Usually a blown cutter head needs to be shipped out to LA, there's a guy out there who fixes them. But luckily, the cutting engineer George knew that National Record Productions (NRP) across the street from TMR in Nashville had a spare cutter head, that was mono, which was not the original intention, but it was the solution that presented itself eighteen hours before we were going to cut it live. I came in the next morning. 'Hey, guess what happened last night?' The cutter head was there in a pile of spare parts. I found out about the problem and the solution at the exact same time."

Obviously, it's not the ideal way for the general overseer who's responsible for the big picture to learn of such a potential event-ending issue, but crisis averted. Blackwell reveals that White handles stress in a situation like this well. "Jack's usually like 'we'll figure it out.'" Ben admits that the Fastest Record on the Plant could not have taken place if it weren't for Third Man's special relationship with United to make these things happen after doing business for five years.

"United probably got more negativity out of it. Every [URP] customer said, 'Well, you turned around a record in a day. Why is it taking six months for our records?' Third Man basically paid to have the plant open and running on a day it would otherwise be closed. That was part of the process. We sold those singles for thirty dollars each, a bit of a markup from what you usually charge for a seven-inch single. It would have been impossible to do without [URP] fully signing on and fully engaging. Our goal was to try to press as many as we could that day. I think we ended up with maybe 800, no more than 900 pressed. I don't think we got to a thousand."

A twenty-first century Rube Goldberg hack of having backup lacquers on standby saved the day, Blackwell explains.

"As soon as the record was cut, we took the lacquer to URP. And then Wes Garland, who was National Record Production's assistant cutting engineer at the time, ran the master tape over to the NRP studio, which is literally right across the street from Third Man. Wes cut a second set of lacquers for speed purposes. We were one-stepping the lacquers. The quickest way to form a metal stamper is directly off of a lacquer. But what happens is if that fucks up, if you fuck up all your one stepping, you can't try again? You have to start from scratch and cut a whole new lacquer. So we knew we were working in a very volatile process. And so we got the second set of lacquers cut one step those that worked and then the first set of lacquers we were able to like crazily make a second set of stampers off so we had it, we actually had the record pressing on three seven-inch presses at the time, so we were able to get a larger number. [Otherwise] we probably wouldn't have had enough for everyone who came that day. I have a very very distinct memory that day of probably around six o'clock or so. The line outside kind of died down. Not one person walks up to the door to get the record. We realize 'No one's here. Close the store before more people show up and we run out of records.' But everyone who came to the store during operating hours got a copy of the single. That promise was probably the hardest thing to keep."

Spillers, Cardiff, UK; Rough Trade, London, UK; Looney Tunes, Long Island, New York; and Fingerprints, Long Beach, California

Phil Collins is known for performing at both Live Aid locations of the July 13, 1985, globally televised charity gig for African famine relief, getting flown via helicopter from Wembley Stadium to Heathrow Airport in London to catch a supersonic Concorde jet to New York City then helicoptered to John F. Kennedy Stadium in Philadelphia.

But on Record Store Day on April 19, 2018, Mike Peters, leader of the Scottish band The Alarm, topped Collins's feat by playing as a solo act in Wales, East London, a New York suburb, and Southern California, in one day.

"I was chasing the sun," quips Peters, admitting that transversing nine time zones—GMT to PST—made the stunt possible. "I thought how can we do something that will really raise the bar and do a Phil Collins. But he had the Concorde. Basically that was the idea."

Executive Donna Ross, whose label Concord released an Alarm record for RSD that day, marveled at what Peters achieved because "Mike just had come back from bone-marrow cancer."

Nonplussed talking about his new lease of life three years later, Peters says the doctors are used to his "mad schemes" and never told him not to do it. While he received a medical all-clear, Jules Peters, his wife, manager, and bass player, initially went "mental," but agreed to accompany him after he calmly laid out the plan to her and showed that it could be done. Being able to sleep on planes definitely helped, conserving his energy.

> "I've been living with the cancer situation since 1995. So I'm pretty adept at managing the way it works. I relapsed in 2015. But through [the recovery] process, it really set me free and allowed me to go on the Vans Warped Tour. I thought if I can survive the Vans Warped Tour, we can survive a twenty-four-hour transatlantic Record Store Day tour."

The Alarm has had seventeen Top fifty UK hits with more than five million in album sales worldwide in the band's thirty-five-plus year career. Peters has been long involved in Record Store Day and often plays British record shops. The 2018 transatlantic jaunt started at Spillers, the world's oldest record shop, having been established in 1894. "I then actually drove to London to play Rough Trade where the fans were waiting to get their records the next day, entertain them for an hour or so in the street. They kind of gave me a big send-off." Peters was driven to Heathrow Airport, and he jumped on the plane to JFK Airport in New York City. "I knew I was going back in time, so I could gain a few hours with each plane journey. And it would allow me to play in the UK, then play in suburban New York, and then play in southern California on the same twenty-four-hour cycle."

For RSD 2018, not only did Concord release a limited edition of The Alarm's eight-song EP, *Where the Two Rivers Meet*, Peters also made six copies of a one-sided single for the occasion, one each for each of the four stores, while one went to an Alarm Fan Club member, and one he kept for himself.

After landing at New York's JFK International Airport, Peters was driven forty miles to Karl Groeger Jr.'s Looney Tunes Records in West Babylon, Long Island, after which he took a JFK flight to LAX, where he was driven to Long Beach to play Rand Foster's Fingerprints Records.

OFFICIAL SEAL OF · RECORD STORE DAY · AMBASSADOR

CHUCK D
2014

DID WE SAY WE WERE honored? *That word barely even covers it.*

Over twenty-seven years and ninety-three countries visited, as a professional lead vocalist of the rap group Public Enemy, I don't go one single day without emphasizing that the genre of hip-hop is spawned from DJ culture. The founding members of Public Enemy were, and still are, DJs. The tool and fuel for DJs has forever been recordings. And where these recordings have long connected, with pros and fans alike, has simply been The Record Store, the connection point of listener and the recording.

The introduction of the available recording to the public had opened and webbed the sounds of the world across the planet long before the internet. It has been influential to the creators of so many of the greatest recordings as well, sort of a second rite of passage after the live radio or TV performance. Motown's Berry Gordy had a record store, Elektra founder Jac Holzman had a record store, the STAX label had their Satellite Record Shop right next to their studio. Keith Richards opens a conversation with Mick Jagger as teenagers on a UK train platform because he had a stack of hot blues records in his arms after leaving a shop. Well you should have an idea of what I'm saying here.

The record store made musicians listen beyond themselves. It both complemented and supplemented the radio, in fact the best radio stations in the past followed the vibe of the record stores of their regions, thus growing and nurturing each other. The fans and listener had everything to gain, and if they wanted to get into making music, the Record Store turned into their first school and sonic passport out.

Do not get me wrong, I am a fan of technology. But I am a bigger fan of the music. I used to be a big fan of the music industry when it, like sports, at least offered a seemingly fair field of play, no matter where one came from. Upon the growth of hip-hop through vinyl-cassette-CD-MP3, I long wanted and advised many Record Stores ways to adapt to surviving the ICE AGE. Like last year's Record Store

Day Ambassador, the great Jack White, I concur with his view that people want to gather, share thoughts, and suggest music. There are few musical events more exciting than Record Store performances, whether it's Grimey's in Nashville, Criminal Records in Atlanta, or Rough Trade in London. I've long thought the Record Store Tour Circuit is so necessary and rewarding.

In this age where industry has threaded the music sound with virtual sight and story, I am honored to be called upon to be Record Store Day Ambassador of 2014. With the masses, neck bent into their smartphones, let all of us music lovers GPS our way into a reality that is the Record Store. It's worth a great try, let's do this....

—Chuck D, 2014 Record Store Day Ambassador

CHAPTER ELEVEN
You Can't Always Get What You Want

"Record prices increase because the manufacturers have not yet found the price at which the market will rebel...."
—Dave Marsh, *Rolling Stone* (1978)

[Record Store Day navigates complaints about high prices, too much product, too little product, and does its best to extinguish flippers on eBay.]

"PEOPLE CAN BE MEAN," KURTZ explains, even acting out over a relatively innocuous entity like Record Store Day. "The second year somebody even sent me what appeared to be a bag of shit in the mail to show me how unhappy they were," adds Kurtz, who never found out who sent the package to his then home address in Silver Lake, Los Angeles. While shocked, he plowed ahead with the mission.

So some retailers remained upset, while consumers also complained about RSD releases' high prices, the big number of releases, so-called "flippers" listing RSD titles on eBay even before they actually had them to sell, not to mention jacking up prices as if it was some sort of speculative commodity that belonged on Wall Street. Definitely not cool and in violation of Record Store Day's unwritten ethos. More formalized "rules" were needed, which is tricky considering RSD being "an open source" event of sorts. Still RSD needs to be somewhat protective of the culture, the brand, and the trademarked words and logo.

Jon Berger, owner of Broadtime, which runs recordstoreday. com, points out that RSD has been successful in getting retailers to pledge they will abide by the rules, such as not posting records for sale in advance of RSD, or jumping the online time that it would be permissible. And even if an RSD release is still unsold months later a participating store will not sell it for more than 20 percent of the original suggested price. In 2021, there were 1,284 Pledge-Signed stores in the US, up from 848 in 2013.

Carrie Colliton monitors and responds to incoming emails to "contact us" at recordstoreday.com. "I try to get a head start by dealing with customer experiences as they're happening. Yeah, we get a lot of social media messages or people who are just kind of bitching on social media in the comments section. But I find that if you show them that you're paying attention to a complaint, such as this record skips, you're able to go in and say, 'Hey, we can help you with that. Email us here.' It's important that people think of Record Store Day in a positive way. And those little interactions are important and helpful because if they think of Record Store Day in a positive way, that means they're thinking of the stores in a positive way. And that's really our whole goal. The [RSD] mission is to shine a positive light on the store."

Sometimes that's not so easy, especially when complainers and haters "don't care and they don't understand that the goal is to support the record stores. It's about, 'You guys fucked up and I didn't get that record'. It's a lot easier for me to be truthful and say, 'I didn't get the record I wanted either.' I don't know if they believe me when I say that, but I feel better knowing they know."

Music fans who complain about the relatively high prices of some Record Store Day releases, points out Colliton, don't realize the economics behind licensing.

"A lot of those reissues have to be relicensed and that's expensive. We want the labels to put some love into the packaging, so that usually costs more money. On the flip side of that, customers complain the prices are too high. Meanwhile, the margins are slimmer for the label, the [independent] distributor, the one-stop [distributor that carries everything and services all outlets], and the store. You're not supposed to be making a regular margin on these records because you also have to factor into that, what they're getting the greatest marketing campaign ever that stores do not pay for directly. So, yes, some store may make less margin on some titles, but what is [Record Store Day] bringing you as a whole? Do you have more customers to super serve and are you going to make more money on everything else in your store that day that you know that you are making bigger margins?"

Retailers complain about not receiving enough RSD product, despite whatever they request from their distributors. For example, by RSD's third year in 2010, Amoeba head buyer Brad Schelden realized that they weren't getting nearly the quantity of each RSD release that it ordered. "For example, I'd request five hundred copies of something, and get only five."

Kurtz says the subject of Record Store Day allocations has always been tricky.

"We have a group of about ten seasoned record store owners who are quite good at determining what a Record Store Day release's production run should be. We give this feedback to artists and labels and then work out the final number. Often they take our advice, but in some cases they will specify that they want a lower number than we would like because they want the record to be truly limited. Beyond that, Record Store Day records are made by hand and there is so much human involvement in the process that the actual quantities that are produced versus what we planned for can vary as much as plus or minus twenty percent."

The sheer volume sometimes is hard for stores to manage, Kurtz admits. "People get stressed out about having to decide how many copies to buy [once the list] gets above three hundred titles, and some record stores order only two hundred or one hundred to make it more manageable for them."

Waterloo Records' John Kunz comments that allocations have "gotten a lot better. I think the record labels have done a better job of communicating with Record Store Day and indicating with stores about how many copies they should make of something." The danger lies in one-stops (distributors that carry all labels) and distributors (which carry only specific labels) sitting on unsold Record Store Day stock from years past. "If [a label] thinks we're gonna sell five thousand and then they only sell three thousand there are still two thousand out there spread around different record stores, one-stops and distributors sitting that never left the warehouses," he adds.

Spencer Hickman, who launched RSD in the UK and now operates his own store, advises retailers not to overextend themselves financially. "I always feel that the best way to approach Record Store Day as a smaller store is to not go too far out of your wheelhouse. You know, like, if you'd never sell an Abba album, why would you order fifty copies of an Abba twelve-inch?" he asks rhetorically. In Hickman's view, whatever number of units that tiny stores like his carry of new vinyl helps them collectively.

> "Record Store Day certainly helped encourage those stores to get back their toes into the vinyl world. [For many,] panic set in because CD sales started to dip and you're like, 'Shit, what am I gonna do? My entire store is CD based and now CD sales are falling.' The amount of press that Record Store Day was getting gave smaller stores confidence to stock vinyl again."

A misconception about Record Store Day is that participating retailers must commit to laying out all kinds of money on records without the option to return if they're not purchased, Colliton notes.

"There are no minimum requirements that force stores to purchase X number of units. In fact, a store can still participate in RSD without selling any of the new special releases. A few stores, who do not sell new products, celebrate Record Store Day by having giant used [record] drops. We realize the list is large, and it covers a lot of genres. And yes, there are stores who are going to bring in everything. But that's not really what it's designed for. If you're a punk rock store, find the punk rock stuff. If you're a metal store, find the metal stuff. Celebrate what you do all-year-long on Record Store Day. So if your store primarily sells used, celebrate that. The releases are just one part of Record Store Day. Yes, [the limited editions] are the giant elephant in the room and the thing most people love and complain about. But that wasn't, they're not the genesis of Record Store Day. And weird as it sounds, they're still not necessarily the heart of it. I wrote an email yesterday to a store where I said the margins are slim on Record Store Day for a lot of reasons. There are fewer of them because they're not wide releases, which means they're going to be more expensive because fewer of them are made."

Warner exec responds to complaints

Billy Fields, Warner Music Group's "vinyl guy," notes that it took a few years for eBay to crack down on the listings. "The evolution of the eBay conversation started with companies going to eBay saying, 'You are allowing people to present on your platform, they have these goods and they do not possess them,'" explains Fields, whose business card gives him the title of vice president of sales, but he added recently to his email signature VP of sales, account management, and vinyl strategist.

"The entire company understands I'm the vinyl expert. When people have questions, they invariably come to me.

Part of eBay rules is you can't put something up for sale on eBay, unless you possess it. Right? You can't guarantee something for sale that you don't have in your possession. That went through a few different iterations, eBay saying, 'No, we're not pulling it down.' eBay finally figured out that in order for them to keep this business selling vinyl on eBay, they needed to be more cooperative with the segment of the business that's driving most of the interest. All these record stores may not be selling on eBay, although a ton of them are, but they're absolutely driving the interest in it. Why would you want to ostracize a huge group of people that are driving interest in people coming to your platform to buy records? I mean, one of the things he basically says is like, they sell a record every forty seconds, or some crazy-ass stat like that, which is probably true. But that's not a new record. That's just a record. That's not driving the new side of the business. But it certainly is helping keep people employed selling records, both new and used. And there's also bootlegs or counterfeit goods and all that kind of shit still goes on."

Fields has been with WMG for twenty-six years in various capacities, starting as an account merchandising rep. Aside from a few years in the mid-2000s working as a VP at then-indie label Rykodisc (since absorbed into WMG), he returned to Warner just after the first Record Store Day happened.

Since Year Two in 2009, a typical complaint against RSD is the sheer number of Record Store Day releases coming out at one time. While WMG has a pretty good track record of putting out quality RSD reissues composed of outtakes or concerts or albums/singles not previously available on vinyl from the likes of Neil Young, The Ramones, The Kinks, The Cure, The Pretenders, Dr. John, Prince, Richard Hell & the Voidoids, Grateful Dead, Tom Petty (*Kiss My Amps*, previously unreleased live tracks), Luna, and Lou Reed, and lost vault jewels by Tiny Tim and Baby Huey, that's not always the case.

"We've done plenty of stuff that's not great. We've done plenty of things that I can't believe we put out. And I tried to stop it, but it's coming out anyway. Some RSD titles at least attempt to hit the mark, while others miss. At least I think we're attempting to hit the mark to begin with." Sometimes important reissues skimp on the packaging and consider a lyric sheet enough to justify the premium price. Fields explains:

> "Actually, a lot of people have said that about the Fleetwood Mac [RSD] alternative records that we put out. It's just the record in a jacket. There's a little bit of notation on the jackets about the tracks. I asked [sometimes for] an insert that provides details about the songs. It's always a slippery slope. And as soon as you get into that kind of conversation, then you're dealing with four or five different artists, possibly, or four or five different managers, possibly, and then everyone's like, 'Well, that's not how we remember it.' It very quickly [gets away] from this is a really cool thing that maybe can get done. I don't want to make that sound like artists are difficult or unreasonable. Feelings change about things. And everyone has their right, especially the artists who have produced the goods to make sure that it's presented in a way that they remember. Do you work toward getting the cool thing that you can get delivered? Or do you spend some extra time and possibly fall down a chasm of trying to get delivered the best thing you possibly can? That's always the balance between human resources and so many creative people. You've got so much stuff to manage."

The quantity for the RSD release of Fleetwood Mac's *Alternative Rumours,* Fields admits, was "just a huge mess on our part. How did we come up with just seven thousand? That's just the wrong number.

What happened? How did we do that? And I don't know how. We took orders of twelve thousand on that. When that happens, you think, 'What's the next thing that we can do?'"

Still it's hard to position something as "super limited edition and collectible when you make fifty thousand of it worldwide. No. It becomes something that is going to be online for years to come from resellers. You want to put as many of these releases into the hands of the fans and minimize how many of these records get into the hands of the people that don't give a shit."

Fields admits the business is always a balancing act, even under ideal circumstances. "How much do you put towards getting all the tapes to all the recordings? Let's make sure we get it mastered correctly. You just have no idea what it takes to make a really good record. And the work that goes into it is at times overwhelming. You know, it's a miracle, frankly, to me at this stage." Fields explains that Vinyl 2.0 couldn't have happened if the majors didn't hold steadfast against accepting returns (i.e., retailers would have to be smart with their ordering). Prices may appear high to consumers, but there's not a lot of wiggle room. In addition, it's not always the majors' fault if insufficient quantities hit the supply chain and make it to the indie stores.

> "There's no way to be profitable if you touch these records more than a couple times. When the entire industry was built upon making vinyl, like back in the original days, every major had their own pressing plants and distribution networks. Every major could control their costs in a way that is completely outside their grip. Now, no one owns their own manufacturing, no one owns their own distribution. We're all relying on third parties. [Compared with] the numbers that were produced then, we're just an afterthought as far as the number of units."

Today's vinyl economics—even exceeding the revenue derived from far greater volumes of CDs—generally don't impress the majors.

"It's a really small amount of revenue. When the numbers are as small as they are like you can't afford to give away returns percentage points and discounting percentage points. In obsolescence, like all the things, you have to do to manage your inventory. When you look at the economics of vinyl, what an unsigned artist has to do to make one hundred records, you get a very quick understanding of why this can't happen," Fields explains.

The first couple of years of Record Store Day, his WMG job didn't involve him in that activity, but he realized, "Hey, this could be good" for getting people interested in vinyl again. "The sales people would ask, 'What should we be putting out?'" In due time, WMG began to mine its deep catalog of the likes of legacy artists Joni Mitchell and The Doors, for example, and even sometimes vinyl boxed sets, Fields notes.

> "The Doors' management, Jeff Jampol, has really been engaged in Record Store Day for a long time for its 'brand.' The Doors' [full catalog] came out in a boxed set, but then it was 'Hey, we need to get all these individual records out.' They'd start doing things like, 'Cool, we'll put out a mono version of the first Doors record, which had not been out since the initial pressing [in late 1966].'"

In contemplating what it can make new on vinyl, WMG's Rhino had released on CD via its own website back in the 1990s direct-to-consumer a series of Doors live shows on the band's "Bright Midnight" imprint. They were never available to retail previously, and made for the perfect RSD titles, Fields points out. "There are these shows and first rehearsal, second rehearsal at the Aquarius. 'Hey, let's go ahead and put that stuff out.' Then they started playing around with [guitarist] Robby Krieger's favorite ten tracks, and [drummer] John Densmore favorite tracks, curated as Record Store Day pieces."

Sometimes negotiations stall with key roster artists—two come to mind but Billy prefers not to name them for the book—but the good news is eventually records did get released. It's Fields's job to figure out all the things needed to be done, asking questions like: "What's in the queue? What needs to be pressed? What does the [sales] forecast look like? What do we have to make? What's the right price? What's the pricing strategy? Where can these be shipped or sold? Let's make sure that we're on schedule. Do we need to submit them to Michael [Kurtz]?"

Most WMG's titles for RSD are catalog reissues, although some artists have put out new music on vinyl that day.

> "The hard part about scheduling a new release for Record Store Day is that new release dates move, they change, plans change, things have to be pushed back. So it's really hard to just align a brand-new record up for the day. I'm not saying it's impossible; I'm just saying it's not an easy task to pull off, and it happens. Sometimes a new release just happens to come out the Friday prior to Record Store Day. That's happened to us a lot. Like we've had Mastodon and Flaming Lips do that before."

Sometimes what's on the shelves for RSD isn't always the choice of the proprietors. Indie stores have become accustomed to realizing they're not necessarily going to receive what they order, sometimes nowhere near. Marc Sendik, owner of High Fidelity Records & CDs in Amityville, New York, in an interview with the online publication VinylWriter.com recently chimed in about the uncertainty of Record Store Day orders.

> "RSD allocations have become pretty brutal but I think that may be because of more shops that opened. Who knows? But when you order fifty of something and get three and there are twelve thousand of them out there—it's a tough pill. I still love the day though! Hey, Record Store Day people who make it happen—I still love you. What really grinds my gears? Iron Maiden doing an exclusive with… WALMART…WTF! [But all in all,] RSD is a good day and

[he loves] seeing passion in people's eyes. It also gets people out buying music, so no complaints."

Karl Groeger, Jr., owner of nearby Looney Tunes, in West Babylon, New York, is more succinct: "RSD has been the godsend for ALL indie record stores." As he recently told VinylWriter's Andrew Daly, "I think [Record Store Day] is an absolutely fantastic organization, and we are proud to be part of it. There will always be haters, but they are just being silly. It's a wonderful event each year and run by amazing people who we care a lot about."

OFFICIAL SEAL OF

BRANDI CARLILE

20 20

RECORD STORE DAY · AMBASSADOR

I'M BRANDI CARLISLE HERE IN Seattle with the twin brothers Tim and Phil Hanseroth. For over two decades, we've been making physical manifestations of independently minded music at the Attic Recording Studio that we built with our own hands. Right now we're listening to Sir Elton John's Madman Across the Water *on vinyl. He's my greatest hero of all time. When he's on tour or when he's at home, he goes into independent record stores and he picks up an armload of records. We have never made an album that we didn't put on vinyl or intend to be in an independent record store.*

Tim's favorite record is Harvest *by Neil Young. He considers it his most beloved record, and he owns several copies picked up over the years at independent record stores. He first discovered it in his mother's record collection when he was a teenager and remembers it instantly transporting him to the 1970s.*

Phil has a very large collection of vinyl, maybe over a thousand records. Most of them were picked up on the road, touring the last fifteen or twenty years, going around to independent music stores. He loves talking to the person behind the counter, finding new stuff. You cannot find these stories online. It's really important to him to have a physical copy aesthetically and super important to support independent retailers.

Blue by Joni Mitchell from 1972 is one of my favorite albums of all time. I have my mother-in-law's copy, which has somebody's memories of it. The record made its way all the way across the Atlantic Ocean to live here in Seattle with me and Catherine. My copy of that album all these years later was signed by the queen—Joni—herself. It's not just an album by Joni Mitchell. These are somebody's dreams in here, and what you hear coming through your speakers. And what independent record stores do is they mine, archive, love, meticulously care for, and make available to you other people's dreams. And that is why it gives me great pride to tell you that we are this year's Record Day Store Ambassadors. Thank you so much for recognizing this love and giving us this opportunity. We won't let you down. Support your independent record stores, keep them open for our kids and for our music.

—Brandi Carlisle, 2020 Record Store Day Ambassador

CHAPTER TWELVE

Rebel Rebel

"I get by because of the people who make a special effort to shop here Saturdays—young men, with John Lennon specs and leather jackets and armfuls of square carrier bags...."
—Nick Hornby, *High Fidelity*, 1995

THE SOUND GARDEN'S BRYAN BURKERT remembers the first Record Store Day in 2008 as "a lot of men with ponytails in high income groups lined up. Over time, that dramatically changed. Now, it's the same men with their daughters. If boys would stop playing video games and buy vinyl, they'd realize all the cool girls are buying vinyl."

CIMS' Andrea Paschal was one of those cool young women back in the day, fighting stereotypes. At twenty-one, she once stood in for Natalie Portman, who was doing a *Star Wars*–related photoshoot in Birmingham by Annie Leibowitz for *Vanity Fair* magazine. Andrea worked at an Alabama record store in 2001, where she met her future husband, Ben (they married in 2016), who also worked there and was initially skeptical of her musical knowledge, even though she played keyboards. Andrea's then-partner Nick was an audio engineer. "When people would come to our house, they would assume it was his record collection they were sifting through," she remembers. "So many people would be like, 'Oh my God, I love this record.' And they tell Nick, 'Man, you got such an amazing record collection.' He'd be like, 'All this is [Andrea's].'"

Guestroom Records' Lisa Foster, who left behind academia in Oklahoma to open a record store in Kentucky with her husband, sees sexist "gender injustice" not only running through society at large but also record stores. A 2009 RSD US survey dispelled stereotypes of who was interested in buying vinyl, finding that among the study's 5,600 RSD participants, 46 percent of them were female.

In May 2016, at the Music Biz convention in Nashville, RSD organizers hosted a town hall for participating record store owners where it became clear that the community of record stores would need to change and be more inviting to women in the industry. At the same time, the people running the coalitions and Record Store Day began to realize that there wasn't anything like the Music Biz convention that was specifically for record stores, where topics like inclusion could be talked about in-depth. They'd need to make their own, expanding on the idea of Noise in the Basement and the ever-expanding meetings that the coalitions each had. What eventually became Record Store Day Summer Camp, a business-to-business convention built around record stores, was executed by the women in the coalitions.

> "Carrie and I had been working together more and more over the years on various projects like Record Store Day stuff proper," says Andrea Paschal of CIMS. "We had just forged a friendship and working relationship. I had done so many conventions in the past, and Carrie had done quite a few things with the Noise in the Basement. Obviously, we were the two people kind of naturally put in charge of like, let's bring all three coalitions together for a Summer Camp."

The idea, and the name, had actually come out of a meeting years earlier in New York City, where all three coalitions got together to talk with major labels. (Summer always seems to be the easiest time for record stores to get together, so the idea of a "summer camp" made sense.) They were together, but still separate, and the gathering that Colliton and Paschal, along with Luann Myers at AIMS, had in mind would be playful but make a point: indie record stores are important independent businesses. Gathering them all together to learn from each other and from experts in business, not just in the music business, strengthens them as single stores, and as an impressive whole as well. Colliton thinks this was one of the most evident examples of how Record Store Day was morphing to fit the needs of the stores it started out to celebrate. "A lot of people think of a record store as this kind of haphazard thrown-together party of a place, where everything is fun and just sort of happens, and there's always a lot of singing and dancing through the aisles, putting out new records. A lot of people who open record stores think of them that way. And there is a LOT of truth in that, but underneath, they are businesses. With overhead, and budgets, and staffing, and human resources concerns, and emergencies just like any other business. And if you got into running a store because 'that record changed my life and I want to do that for others,' that's amazing and magical but you may not be as well versed in the other stuff as you need to be. That's where we hoped Summer Camp could come in a little. But you can't get together without having a lot of fun, because the people of record stores won't stand for that, so we left a lot of room for the singing and dancing in the aisles part."

The first Summer Camp marked a return to Baltimore, and when it came time to choose the location for the second, Raleigh, North Carolina, where Colliton is based, and where the first SparkCon meetings took place seemed like a good fit. Venues and hotels were chosen, and contracts almost signed when House Bill 2, a bill that required transgender people to use public restrooms that corresponded with the gender on their birth certificates, passed.

"A lot of record store owners didn't want to go because they just didn't want to support a state that was passing this. Record stores are supposed to be a safe space for people, where all the outliers and misfits, where we all kind of flocked to, right? Bruce Springsteen cancelled his concert in North Carolina, the NBA pulled the All-Star Game. Ultimately, we decided to head back to Baltimore and planning a conference for hundreds of people in about a month and a half wasn't easy, but it was the right thing to do," says Colliton.

Eventually, Summer Camp found a home at the independently run Hotel Monteleone in New Orleans, and grew from year to year, with the support of the music industry and businesses from all aspects of the record store world. "What helped cement the [Summer Camp] idea that this could be cool to do was because you had people from different realms of the same musical universe together," says Paschal. "Something in the back of our minds was to have Record Store Day be more inclusive of other record stores as well like we're trying to grow this event."

The natural effect brought about by this expanded inclusivity became immediately apparent in that there were no more panel discussions run exclusively by men, and one of the first, and most popular, presentations at Summer Camp came from Lisa Foster of Guestroom Records, who laid out for a lot of well-meaning, eager-to-learn male record store owners what making a store inviting to female customers would look like (hint: who's in the posters on your walls? It's not JUST about cleaning the bathroom, but for goodness sake, clean the bathroom!) and got a standing ovation. Four years later, record stores report that more than 50 percent of people who celebrate Record Store Day are women while multiple Grammy Award–winning singer-songwriter Brandi Carlile, whose music spans many genres, took on the role as Record Store Day's Ambassador. "A few years ago," says Colliton, "I was in a record store about a week before Record Store Day, and I saw a young Black woman (she looked like a teenager) walk up to the counter with a metal record in her hand and ask the guy behind the counter what time they'd be open on Record Store Day. This blew so many different stereotypes out of the water that even then I was thinking, 'Am I being set up? Is this actually what's happening?' I wanted to cry and run up to her and ask her to be in a commercial or something, but she had a new record to go home and listen to, and I was honestly afraid I might cry all over her, so I wisely left her alone."

Over in the UK, RSD coordinator Kim Bayley also observed a shift in what the average record store customer looks like.

> "It's a lot more equal nowadays between men and women who are out on Record Store Day. There is something for everyone on that list. There's something which welcomes you in and makes you want to be a part of something bigger than you know. In the past, record shops were seen as being a bit dusty and very male dominated, and maybe a little bit intimidating. We've definitely got lots more shops owned by women nowadays that are very welcoming. The customers are female."

According to 2021 research by the UK's Entertainment Retailers Association, more than 60 percent of the more than 140 RSD-participating British record store owners reported growing numbers of women coming into their stores and enjoying the vinyl experience. Ashlie Green, who helps run David's Music in Letchworth, England, provided more evidence of women's interest in buying physical music.

> "Record shops have had a history of being fairly male-dominated spaces—but the *High Fidelity*-esque days (referring to the 1990s novel and movie) are definitely over as more and more women are enjoying vinyl. Not only are there more women behind the counter but the spaces themselves are much more welcoming to all people of all ages. Record Store Day is a great driver for that too as the list of releases is so eclectic and brings in music lovers from every background for what is normally a big party!"

Recognizing that more young women were interested in Record Store Day, on March 4, 2020, just before the pandemic quarantined the world, organizers announced The Big Moon, a four-piece girl band from London, as the UK's RSD Ambassadors for 2020. RSD UK coordinator Megan Page commented at the time that, "The Big Moon speaks more to that sixteen-to-twenty-four-year-old younger woman audience." For the launch event, The Big Moon played a special set recorded live to vinyl at Metropolis Studios in West London, attended by one hundred lucky fans who were given headphones to hear what the engineer and the producer upstairs was saying to the band at the time. They did three tracks in one take, including a cover of Fatboy Slim's "Praise You," and the resulting twelve-inch came out on Record Store Day. Of course, it sold out.

CHAPTER THIRTEEN

Shake It Off

*"It was pretty clear what was happening and
April didn't seem like a good idea."*
—Carrie Colliton

*[2020–2021: Record Store Day participating stores increase sales even
during Covid-19.]*

Planning for the 2020 Record Store Day began full of optimism. On January 6, 2020, Colliton and Kurtz were at the Consumer Electronics Show in Las Vegas with longtime RSD supporters Crosley to launch the transparent RSD 3 turntable made for Post Malone's 3" records, and to announce that the thirteenth Record Store Day was coming April 18, 2020. Post Malone was dominating the charts, and record stores were happy selling a lot of his CDs.

In February, Colliton and Kurtz were in Dallas meeting with record store owners, plotting special events, and talking about the upcoming special RSD releases. A week later they were with all the RSD organizers in New York crammed together in a great little bar talking about Record Store Day, the year ahead and its future. On March 5, RSD announced online the 2020 title list, which Kurtz promoted on air with Sirius XM radio. Things were going well.

"It was a fantastic list, one of the best lists in a long time, and it was really well received from the start, which doesn't always happen with [RSD] lists, sometimes they have to grow on people."

Colliton admits. "People were really looking forward to it. And then we started having conversations the next week internationally."

Italy was one of the first pandemic hotspots and were already closed down, as were other places throughout Europe, and the news about something called "Covid-19" was growing more and more ominous in the United States. The mood darkened.

"It was pretty clear something was happening and all of sudden April didn't seem like a good idea," Colliton continues. "We're looking ahead a couple of months in the calendar, but it's very hard to make decisions for the world in advance [not knowing what direction Covid could take]. It looks like magic when records show up in record stores. But that's not the case. They have to get pressed; they have to get packaged; they have to get shipped; they have to get ordered; they have to get allocated; they have to get to the stores. So we had to make these decisions with enough time for all of that to be moved around."

The ramifications of delay would impact everyone along the supply chain. For example, what happens to an indie label's title planned and prepared for April, but it's put on hold for an unclear amount of time. "There's real money tied up in that," Colliton notes. "[RSD] can't ask them to sit on that forever." By mid-March, the US started locking down, forcing most stores to close their doors indefinitely. On March 13, RSD announced the new global date would be moved to June 20. "At the time, that felt like a pretty realistic decision," Colliton explains. "We're going to sit for a little while. See what's happening. See if lockdowns work, see if people will wear masks. Warm weather was supposed to knock that sucker out. Maybe things will be fine in June. So let's plan for that. Pretty quickly after that, Europe says that's not going to work. If we are all about supporting indie record stores, then supporting them through the pandemic is going to be even bigger. So June was probably not going to work [for everybody worldwide] on a single day because it's in the public interest to close their stores or because they actually had

Covid on staff, or because a local mandate or state mandate has said you are a non-essential business and you need to close. So you're looking at stores for two or three months maybe with no revenue, and there's no idea of what the revenue is going to be like after that. Don't forget that Record Store Day doesn't give the titles to the stores. The stores place their orders and purchase them. If you've come out of three months of reduced [from online sales] or no revenue, even if it's the greatest list, that's a really scary prospect. Then there are the optics: You don't want to have a single day where you're encouraging thousands of people to come down to the place, stand in line to get records [and potentially catch the disease]."

Kurtz credits Colliton for coming up with the "three drops" concept. The decision to break up the list into three days later in the year (August 29, September 26, and October 24) came after conversations with stores, labels, and distributors, all the pieces that work together resulting in records for Record Store Day. Instead of "drops" they considered calling them "street dates," but in Europe that term means nothing. "So we had to think of something that made sense, was still kind of fun, and worked internationally. You can't really call it Record Store Day because it's not," Carrie explains. "And you don't want three Record Store Days. All these decisions have to be made, but at the same time, you have to protect, for lack of a less annoying word, the brand that is 'Record Store Day,' which is the day in April. You don't want to water it down. You don't want to call these 'Record Store Days' because they're not. We wanted to be very clear. We're not encouraging parties. We're not encouraging crowds. We're not encouraging bands and everything that has come associated with Record Store Day [in the past]."

Making the decision was "kind of terrifying from the inside," Colliton admits. "There were uncomfortable conversations and emails between Record Store Day organizers worldwide. Some stores thought, and still think, it wasn't a good idea. Others thought, 'This could maybe work, it'll probably be much smaller.

I guess we'll see.' What happens if someone on your staff gets Covid? What happens if someone gets sick? What happens if a customer refuses to play by your rules? (e.g., wearing a mask)."

Other stores thought they should just shut it down for the year, or just allow everybody to sell everything online, which would leave out a lot of stores who for years were staunchly brick-and-mortar and refused to compete with the internet. "That's a perfectly fine way to run your brick-and-mortar business when there's not a pandemic," Colliton notes. Another idea was to let the releases be sold via artist websites. "That wouldn't have really benefited the stores," she notes.

"In addition, RSD couldn't endorse the notion of customers hanging out, talking to other people, touching things, and flipping through the racks, all the things you can't really do in 2020 (or 2021, for that matter). How does a brick-and-mortar record store survive that? Stores rose to the occasion, reaching their customers and making sales in ways that they hadn't before, including online, curbside service, deliveries in vans," Carrie points out.

"That means being super creative. Fortunately, record stores have proven themselves to be creative, nimble, flexible, quick to figure out ways to make twenty percent capacity happen, for example. It really solidified their community and has been such a joyful thing to watch. End of All Music (Oxford, Miss.) took advantage of being on the second floor of their building. They have a balcony that looks out on the square. It's big enough for an artist to play up there. They're very creative; their 'curbside pickup' was a dumbwaiter that they lowered up and down from the balcony to the customers on the ground."

Two months before the first drop, Colliton would hold Zoom calls with twenty-five to thirty stores on each call. "We went over, 'All right, what are we doing? What does your space look like?

Are you able to do appointment shopping? How many people can you get in? How are you doing this? How are you having a day that's all about crowds,'" she explains. Some of the stores have been doing Record Store Day for more than a decade, thinking they have it down to a science, and know how things are set up. "And we're saying you probably can't do any of that. For some of the stores, what it came down to was we just have to get them in and out to buy these records without shopping for everything else. We were very clear with the stores that they may not make as much money on this day—it actually didn't turn out this way for many—as you did last year for so many reasons. You need to be prepared for that."

Realizing that some stores were not able to reopen, or some customers didn't feel visiting a store in person to buy a record was worth taking the risk of being infected, Record Store Day decided to relax the rule of stores being prohibited from selling RSD releases online. "I think it saved a couple stores," Colliton explains.

> "[Allowing online sales earlier than usual] was a global decision. The internet doesn't respect borders. So if the UK starts selling something, somebody from the US can buy it, and vice versa. So it had to be one time, the same time around the world. And that was one p.m. (EST), which stores on the West Coast were not super happy about because people on the East Coast could buy their stuff, and they'd only been open for an hour or two. In March, we were making this decision for August, September, and October. We had no idea what the world is going to be like, who's going to be able to open. We had at least two stores on the first drop in August, who had put their plans in motion to do spaced-out appointment shopping, and then on the Thursday before, they had an employee test positive. They can't open at all. And they've already bought all this product. So we told them 'At one o'clock, go for it, sell it, tell your customers to shop online, or call us and pick it up.' That saved those stores.

They had all this stuff and all these plans, and instantly those plans were out the window; they could not let people in their building. For the October 2020 drop, Ireland shut down with like forty-eight hours notice, so they fans couldn't shop. So the fact that they were able to start selling online at six o'clock is what saved those stores, at least for that day."

Colliton opines, The pandemic gave people "an overwhelming sense of loss, mortality, and nostalgia. And I think that made people kind of cling to the things they love, and the times they love, such as physical books and physical media of all sorts. Pair that with the need to support local, independent businesses. It was shocking to them. I don't think there is a store around that would tell you they expected the year to go the way it did."

It turned out that the three RSD drops were overwhelmingly supported by record store owners and their customers. Collective sales over the 2020's three drops exceeded RSD's April 2019 revenue, with most stores reporting RSD sales up 5 to 10 percent over 2019. "We took it as a sign that the drops were successful and a good idea, but I don't like comparing them to one day because that was one day in April compared to three days in August, September, and October," Colliton notes. Even though they guessed right, Kurtz says the downside was that the emotional rollercoaster "exhausted everybody. It was really hard." Kurtz also notes that the pandemic forced some RSD retailers finally into e-commerce. About 60 percent had already sold online before the March 2020 lockdown.

Amoeba Records' Jim Henderson says the drops "allowed us also to meet new customers because being able to sell online, which was always forbidden until the day after." So that kind of level playing field—if you were in Cincinnati, you could still shop Amoeba on Record Store Day—broadens the shopping experience for all retailers. It was kind of a cool thing. If you look at the positives of [the pandemic], a lot of people got to experience different record retailers on Record Store Day without actually leaving their houses."

Jan Koepke, the RSD coordinator for Germany, Switzerland, and Austria, says the 2020 "three-drop" strategy worked out well.

"It was very much a work in progress and the original plan for the three drops was a little bit different from what happened in the end. The first drop in late August had by far the largest number of RSD items (which was intended to be the other way round). But in the end, the shops and the customers behaved well, kept to the distance rules and were happy that RSD took place—even during the pandemic. The sales in the stores didn't reach the level of any regular RSD of the past, but those shops that have a well-frequented online shop could indeed take advantage from the adjustment of the strict online rules. In the end, it counts what is good for the shops to survive this critical year."

British stores showed similar results despite the pandemic. Vinyl continues to enjoy its thirteenth consecutive year of growth in the UK (which, remember, came in the year after joining Record Store Day) with sales in January to May of this year alone topping more than 1.8 million vinyl albums and surpassing a spend of over £40 million (US$55.8 million)—that's up over 46 percent compared with 2020, announced in a June 2020 press release. "This surge is most likely being driven by a nation being locked inside and having more time than ever before to reconnect with the art and music they love," ERA stated. In 2007, only 75,000 vinyl albums were sold in the UK, but fast-forward to 2020, that number has rocketed to more than five million units and over £110 million (US $153.5 million) in value.

In the end, the global pandemic could not stop vinyl's momentum or Record Store Day. MRC Data (formerly Nielsen) reported that 2020 new vinyl sales increased 46.2 percent with 27.5 million sales in a year that forced independent stores to close, or fundamentally change their way of doing business. And it wasn't just the pandemic that altered record stores in 2020. There was more to do.

A Change is Gonna Come

In the summer of 2020, George Floyd's video-recorded murder by police galvanized social protests globally. In response, on June 2, 2020, the music industry at large acknowledged the work of Jamila Thomas and Brianna Agyemang and their demand that the "Show Must Be Paused." Everyone in the music business was asked to pause for twenty-four hours and rethink their relationship with the Black people in their lives: their coworkers, their associates, their partners, their friends.

Michael Kurtz took the day to think about record stores within the music industry. "I had worked with Dedry Jones in Chicago and helped him with his dream to create what he called a 'Music Experience.' Dedry's idea was to create a platform for Black artists to talk about the positive message in Black music." He hosted several legendary Music Experiences in his Chicago store, but sadly, Dedry passed away right before his first "Music Experience" aired on PBS.

Kurtz had also worked with the Urban Network, a coalition of Black owned record stores back in the early 2000s. "Black-owned record stores have always represented something more than just a place to buy music in their communities," Kurtz says. "These businesses have been hubs for social and political activism, self-expression, culture, and belonging. They are at the heart and soul of the music industry and the impact they have had on their communities to push for important social and political progress is immeasurable."

However, Black-owned record stores were disappearing at a rapid rate. "There are only thirty-two left; there used to be hundreds," Kurtz told The Vinyl District in June 2021. "But it's because they got so disenfranchised. We reached out to them, and they were like, 'Nobody's called us in over a decade, from the labels to the music business. We're on our own.'"

Joining forces with footwear and skateboard brand Vans in 2021, Record Store Day responded to the Black Lives Matter zeitgeist with Open Doors, a social media/video campaign highlighting Black-owned record stores and a two-volume RSD vinyl compilation of music from Black artists called "Songs For You." Nineteen artists donated tracks to the album, including H.E.R., Run The Jewels, Curtis Mayfield, Common, Freddie Gibbs & the Alchemist, Pop Smoke, and Lupe Fiasco. Roberta Flack provided a previously unreleased recording of Marvin Gaye's "What's Going On" that perfectly asked why police brutality was still going on in 2021.

The campaign provided videos about five Black-owned record stores, including Brittany's Record Shop in Cleveland and Offbeat Records in Jackson, Mississippi, built in 2014, and it was meant to be as much a community meeting place as a record store that sells music, graphic novels, trade paperbacks, and manga. When asked that the store be used as water hub for the community, "Of course" was the response from Offbeat owner Phillip Rollins. "Growing up, I didn't see any Black people in a comic shop besides me and my mom," Rollins remembers. "As a Black-owned business, I want to make sure that this place is really inclusive and welcoming, especially for people of color, or people who get misgendered. I've heard so many stories about that stuff," he adds. Adrienne Domnick, a Black visual artist, notes that Offbeat served as a gallery for her artwork. "It was the first place that I actually had an exhibit. That opened up many doors that really changed my whole life." In the video, Garrad Lee, a professor of Black History, underscores the importance of businesses like these, pointing out that it's "super empowering for a young black person to own a store, and it's important for us to use our privilege and our money to support those places."

The community hub aspect of all record stores is particularly called out by both the owners and the supporters of all the Black-owned record stores in the Open Doors series. In the video showcasing Retrofit Records in Tallahassee, a customer points out that when a hurricane knocked out power to much of the community, owner Sharod Bines, who had power at Retrofit, invited everyone in to use it. "A person of color owning an independent music store is unfamiliar to a lot of people," says Bines. Retrofit is dispelling myths that a Black person can't like punk, jazz, *and* soul, and Bines' eclectic tastes are reflected in the store stock and customer base. Since opening in 2013, Retrofit has become a pillar in the community, and that is particularly important, according to hip hop scholar Jian Jones, a professor at Florida A&M University. "Black ownership is about keeping that money within your community so we can have better schools, better opportunities. That is why we need Black businesses," Prof. Jones adds.

Record Store Day had previously recognized the importance of Black artists to the culture of record stores and pop culture in general by working to increase the number of Black artists on the official Lists, and naming hip-hop duo Run the Jewels, RSD Ambassador in 2018, and bestowing the sash on rap pioneer Chuck D in 2014, the year after his Public Enemy was inducted into the Rock and Roll Hall of Fame.

One outlet for the vinyl industry to have continued growth is hip-hop. Making more titles available on vinyl makes sense, considering the genre is responsible for 47 percent of the top one hundred albums, yet only 49 percent of those albums are available on vinyl for record stores to stock, points out Carl Mello, Newbury Comics' senior buyer and director of brand engagement. "If you remove catalog and older albums from the list, the percentage of titles available on vinyl falls to around forty percent."

And in the end...

When the idea for Record Store Day was first discussed fifteen years ago, approximately one million vinyl records were sold in the USA, almost all of them audiophile or records pressed for bands to sell on the road. As of the middle of 2021, with Record Store Day bringing together a diverse and engaged community, vinyl sales totaled 21.684 million records for the first six months of the year, up 111.9 percent over the same period in 2020. MRC's count of 1.549 million vinyl records sold during the first RSD 2021 Drop represented an increase of 121.6 percent, compared to the previous week (698,000). That's the second-largest week for vinyl album sales since MRC Data (formerly Nielsen/SoundScan) began tracking sales in 1991. So not only did the RSD Drops 2020 strategy exceed the 2019 Record Store Day sales results, when the Drops idea was extended into 2021 due to lingering pandemic restrictions and supply chain disruptions, the two combined June RSD drops out-performed the combined three RSD Drops of 2020, according to MRC Data, by a couple of hundred thousand vinyl albums. The return of vinyl as the dominant physical media is now complete.

But what happens when music fans can resume fully their pre-Coronavirus lives outside the home bubble they've created? Will their love affairs with their turntables and newly assembled collections be over? My hunch is that once consumers of any age catch the vinyl bug, it's not going to be so easy to give up. One way the industry as a whole could keep its momentum going is by focusing on the increasing number of young people who think vinyl is cool, the record store customers of the future. Releasing more of the new music they're interested in on vinyl, beyond Billie Eilish, Harry Styles, and Phoebe Bridgers, would be a step in the right direction. After all, there is a reason the Lady Gaga and Arianna Grande Record Store Day releases lit up Twitter and TikTok and were on almost all record stores' Top Sellers Lists for the first 2021 RSD Drops date. As Newbury Comics' Carl Mello points out, "If we don't start prioritizing the needs of a younger, more diverse customer base, who do we imagine will be buying vinyl at our stores in 2035?"

MRC data's analysis of the first five months of 2021 showed the tide might be turning regarding a youth movement. The five Top-Selling Vinyl Albums for that period were Harry Styles' *Fine Line,* Kendrick Lamar's *Good Kid, M.A.A.D. City,* Billie Eilish's *When We All Fall Asleep,* Billie Eilish's *Don't Smile at Me,* and Taylor Swift's *folklore.* And when you examine just the albums that were released in 2021, Ariana Grande's *Positions* and Lana Del Rey's *Chemtrails Over the Country Club* are right near the top. This suggests that vinyl today shouldn't be measured against streamed "hits" or the make-or-break, first-week sales mentality that dominated the record industry since the 1970s. Despite the manufacturing and distribution issues that continue to provide challenges in vinyl getting to them, there's empirical evidence that artists' fans will be there when the records hit record stores.

The artists are certainly already there. Sony International's Gerhard Blum points out that you'll be hard-pressed to find an artist who *doesn't* want their music released "day and date," simultaneously on digital (streaming) formats and physical formats, including vinyl. "When an artist goes on a morning TV show for an interview to promote an album, what does the host hold up?" Even if it sometimes means the vinyl isn't always in the stores yet.

Thankfully, even the world's largest record conglomerate, Universal Music Group, recognizes the importance Record Store Day played in resurrecting vinyl. As Michael Kurtz often stresses, artists drive vinyl enthusiasm. Universal Music Enterprises' Sujata Murthy, who oversees Universal Music Group back catalog, agrees. "At times an artist has a very clear vision of what they would like to release [for Record Store Day], and we share in that vision. We are thrilled with the results and continue to actively support RSD and indie record stores throughout the entire year. The ability for indie retail to not only survive but to thrive is crucial to our industry now and into the future. Now that we have plenty of RSD history we take into careful consideration previous RSD releases. Titles are often suggested by artists themselves who have something special in mind to thank fans who shop and support indie retail. We also assess what content is in the UME archives that has potential to be a great RSD title to release. Sometimes the opportunity presents itself to align an RSD release with active roster artist release activity. We are always looking for ways to bridge the gap between new releases by celebrating an artist's catalog. RSD releases perfectly complement ongoing artist activity."

Back in 2007, Kurtz staked record stores' collective future on vinyl. Now he admits that he himself wasn't fully convinced at the time. "I almost lost my job over it because people were like, 'Why are you putting so much work into vinyl? We don't sell vinyl. We sell CDs. There's no business for vinyl.' Record Store Day developed that business."

Bull Moose's Chris Brown can now appreciate that Record Store Day "came around at the right time; the world was ready for records to come back. I think [RSD] reminded people that records are fun. Surely the record companies realized that people wanted these records and started making them again." In a 2014 blog post for Diffuser, Brown went a bit further, explaining what Record Store Day has accomplished.

> "Millions of music fans and thousands of industry and retail folks came together to turn a crazy idea into a magical holiday. We only wanted to have a little fun and celebrate our shared passion for music and records. We wound up giving the music industry the best news it has had in decades and revitalizing an entire format."

Carrie Colliton partly attributes RSD's sustained growth over the past fifteen years simply to the number of stores getting involved.

> "That grew and the number of people who knew Record Store Day grew. More stores are bringing in more people.

They know more about record stores on a general, year-round basis. People love record stores now; it's a pop culture thing. As Record Store Day grew, record stores got a little more confident that they can sell these records, even though they're nonreturnable and limited-edition, they can sell more of these to their customers. Record Store Day is a worldwide event. The largest single-day worldwide music event, when we're allowed to have it on one day. Celebrated in every continent except Antarctica. And that's only because they don't have a record store there. If there was a record store, they'd probably have a party there too."

Beyond succeeding with the original mission of throwing a party to celebrate the culture of record stores and bringing back vinyl, Sound Garden owner Bryan Burkert boils down the success of Record Store Day in simple monetary terms, with results echoed by many other indie stores. "Record Store Day triples the amount of the best sales day I've ever had, which would be the Saturday before Christmas. Record Store Day has changed the industry, changed my store, and the way we do business. After Record Store Day, we had to build an additional room. Our vinyl business tripled and our customer base now crosses generations."

EPILOGUE

IN 1977, FRENCH ECONOMIST JACQUES Attali (author of *Noise: The Political Economy of Music*) predicted Record Store Day's ability to get people to line up the night before with wish lists of limited editions in their pockets, thirty years early: "People buy more records than they can listen to. They stockpile what they want to find the time to hear."

The pandemic raged for over a year, taking the lives of more than half a million Americans by the spring of 2021 and demonstrating how precious our time is on planet Earth. Covid-19 claimed the life of one regular Record Store Day shopper named Tom Burgess, who I never met but consider a kindred spirit for being a music lover and an adjunct professor. I learned of Tom's death because of his record collection of a hundred thousand LPs, representing a who's who of rock, jazz, classical, and world music, being on sale for the first six months of 2021 a block-and-a-half away from where I live in Manhattan's Washington Heights. There were also twice as many books of all genres. Among my RSD finds, originally purchased by Burgess, included a sealed copy of a holy grail, the 2014 release of *Donny Hathaway's Live at the Bitter End 1971*. I knew of the album but never saw it before. It felt almost sacrilegious to obtain it this way. I also bought that day the 2013 RSD release *The Hidden Treasures of Taj Mahal*, which I once saw elsewhere years ago but kicked myself for not adding it to my collection. I picked up Tom's unopened copy of the RSD reissue of *The Dresden Dolls*, although I decided to leave for another crate-digger Flaming Lips' 2013 RSD *Zaireeka* boxed set. I didn't want to come off as too greedy.

As it turns out, Tom and I taught at the same college, CUNY's Borough of Manhattan Community College (BMCC) in downtown Manhattan, although I was there for only the fall semester for English 101, whereas he was there for two decades teaching anthropology and sociology. BMCC is a few blocks away from the large J&R Music World store that closed in 2014.

Before Sam Phillips's 2002 DORS conference speech, the Sun Records founder marveled about his J&R visit earlier in the day. "It totally had the feeling as though you were going to the warmest place on this earth…You could tell that it was run by individuals that love what they are doing and fighting their ass off to make it a place of enjoyment for people to come and spend their money."

Based on all of the J&R bags I found at the pop-up store, Tom spent a lot of money there. I find it most heartbreaking that Tom didn't get a chance to listen to so much of his collection—lots of sealed records remained in unopened J&R bags. Literally dozens of RSD vinyl titles—mostly unopened—dating back to its earliest days showed how Tom embraced the annual holiday year after year. I purchased from his impressive collection about two hundred LPs, a hundred 45s, several dozen CDs, and about half dozen CD boxed sets.

"The first trip I took [to Tom's crammed one-bedroom apartment in upper Manhattan's neighborhood of Inwood], I found a whole shelf of Record Store Day stuff, LPs and singles," remembers Will Glass, who ran the pop-up sale with his wife, Veronica. She founded Word Up, a neighborhood nonprofit bookstore, where Tom often volunteered. The proceeds from the sale of his records and books went to Word Up. The Glasses live in a Washington Heights building that their landlord graciously allowed them to use the vacant space for the first months of 2021 to sell off the massive collection before donating the records and books in a pop-up store known as "Recirculation," named after Burgess's philosophy of donating objects based on the idea that capitalism had already produced enough to go around.

"[Tom] had a thing for collecting stuff that had good value, and some day the ARChive [for Contemporary Music, where Tom also volunteered and donated stuff] could sell it for more," explains Glass, who works at the Jazz Foundation, so he's the perfect individual to preside over such a music endeavor. "I could tell he just enjoyed Record Store Day for the exciting collector side of it," he adds.

Tom and I had a mutual adjunct friend, Jessica Smart, who teaches psychology, and who I once met at a union meeting. She told me that Tom had been suffering from lung cancer for about four years, surmising his condition to BMCC's close proximity to the World Trade Center on 9/11. She notes that adjuncts generally don't have adequate health insurance. I know this firsthand from being inflicted with an extreme case of shingles of the eye and face that hit me literally overnight in February 2021, halfway through writing this book. Two trips to the ER and associated doctor visits, according to Anthem, will cost me out-of-pocket about $5,000, even with health insurance. In any case, the ordeal set back finishing the book by at least a month. Thankfully, I'm on the mend healthwise, but here's a tip: if you had chicken pox when you were a kid and are now over fifty years old, get a shingles vaccine.

In early February 2020, Jessica was surprised to see Tom on campus after he missed a few semesters. She figured his health must have rebounded. Weeks later, the pandemic lockdown occurred, so they never crossed paths again. She still feels guilty about a CD he loaned her, and fondly remembers running into him at a City Winery gig of Dave Davies of The Kinks. "I figured I'd run into you here," she told him. I mentioned to Jessica that I'm also a massive Kinks fan and was also at that show. It's too bad I didn't know either of them at that point.

Live performance and record stores serve as an oasis for human interaction as much as a dive bar if they ever open again. Friendships and romances can be formed as discerning music fans bond over what they already cherish, or discover as revelation, based on what's wafting from the speakers or PA and spinning from the turntable. Any crate-digger who looks forward to the coming Record Store Day asks the seeming philosophical question about why buy on vinyl certain titles that you already own on CD or cassette or both. Is being a format completist necessary?

Jessica Smart wasn't surprised to hear that her friend Tom Burgess amassed an RSD stash. "I think adjuncts need to do what makes them happy." That observation, in a nutshell, is why we collect—and hopefully spin what we purchase on Record Store Day. It makes us happy. Our astral plane awaits.

ACKNOWLEDGMENTS

In a strange way, I have Michael Kurtz's ex-wife to thank for making this book happen. If it weren't for Sheila Valentine responding to something I wrote in 2015 for my former fanzine (the *Walford Gazette*) about the popular British TV program *EastEnders*, I might have never become close friends with Michael. Looking to promote subscription renewals, the subject line of my email blast stated, "Happy Record Store Day," which was coming up the next week. I attached the cover of the 1985-issued seven-inch single of the *EastEnders* theme song and wrote, "If the BBC knew what it was doing, it would reissue this for Record Store Day." Sheila was a subscriber to the *Gazette* and emailed me, "My ex-husband was a cofounder of Record Store Day." She offered to make an introduction. The very next day Michael and I met for coffee in Harlem. Two-and-a-half years later, Michael helped me and my Making Vinyl cofounder Bryan Ekus launch our B2B conference covering the global rebirth of new vinyl manufacturing, an activity I kind of doubt would have happened without Record Store Day brilliantly capturing consumers' fancy, which, in turn, reinvigorated the entire vinyl food chain.

I owe a great deal of gratitude to RSD's Carrie Colliton for sharing her memories, contacts, and rich anecdotes that serve as the foundation of this book.

Some of the writing contained in the proceeding pages had its genesis in the Making Vinyl program guides, a feature for *Long Live Vinyl* about the RSD Summer Camp, and two long feature articles I wrote for Gene Pitts's August journal *The Audiophile Voice*. I suggested in *TAV* in 2016 the vinyl comeback was being grossly underestimated by the powers-that-be but swallowed as gospel by the mainstream media. Gene hails from the old school of journalistic skepticism, and I applaud him for eventually allowing me to make the case that the vinyl resurgence was not only real, but it had traction and was not going away any time soon.

Here's a shoutout to Tim Clair, proprietor of Record Reserve in Northport, New York, who helped me realize in 2012 how much I missed the record store culture of my youth, and like so many other boomers, a place to hang out and learn about music and life. While perusing Tim's dollar bins, I picked out an amazing burlesque jazz record on Cameo Parkway. I felt like Al Pacino in *Godfather 3*, "Just when I thought I was out, they pull me back in!"

I kicked myself for what a big mistake I made in 2010 shedding most of my four thousand-LP and four thousand-CD collection during a decluttering moment of CD digitizing-to-iTunes madness, wrongly concluding that my iPod was sufficient for satisfying my music consumption needs. Over the next eight years, Record Reserve's three dollars used stock recreated much of my original collection, and then some. And the past few years, Tim allowed me to cover for him once a month to taste what it was like to work at a record store (paying me in used records, lol), a job I could never land when I was a teenager.

My hobby started rubbing off on those around me, including my girlfriend, Theta Pavis, whose brother bestowed upon her for Christmas a record player that soon would play an original 45 of The Doors single "Love Her Two Times," which I gave her on date number two. After all, a Jim Morrison poster adorned her walls when she was a teenager. Theta's fifteen-year-old daughter Delphine turned me onto Billie Eilish, who she had been listening to via YouTube well before the release of her debut LP *When We Sleep, Where Do We Go*. I purchased a shrink-wrapped new copy from Tim for Delphine, who marveled over this new contraption in their living room. She excitedly asked, "How do you turn this thing on?" Responding to the magic of playing vinyl, she shared it immediately with her friends on Instagram, giving me hope that Gen-Z might just keep the format alive.

My influence also must have rubbed off on Cybrieme Hargrove and Gabrielle Pinewood, two college students of mine, who are graduating in May 2022 from the New York Institute of Technology. They surprised me in the fall of 2021 with publishing a poem about their separate love affair with vinyl in the campus newspaper I advise. Neither of them were aware of Record Store Day until I told them about this book. For RSD to thrive in the future, it's going to need to reach all the Gabys and Cybriemes of this world. Thanks also to Nicole Pereira, the best NYIT student I ever had, whose tech knowledge led me to Otter for transcriptions, without which I wouldn't be able to finish the book. Nicole was also a great intern for the first Making Vinyl.

During my recent years living on Long Island to assist my ailing, now departed, parents, my respite for a few hours a week was spent at Record Reserve, Karl Groeger's Looney Tunes, High Fidelity, Mr. Cheapos, and Infinity—I'd hit them all on Record Store Day—making my private quandary a bit more more tolerable.

Now ensconced in the more familiar ground of New York City during 2020 and 2021's five RSD drops and Black Friday, I've shared the love at Sharone Bechor's Rock and Soul, Rough Trade, Record Runner, Village Music World, Generation Records, and Cinder Block.

Please allow me to acknowledge all the essential work provided by record store owners, their employees and customers, as well as all the vinyl-focused labels, the mastering and cutting houses, packaging specialists and pressing plants for keeping us sane during these trying times, who make every day Record Store Day. Without you, there wouldn't be much to write about. So to the exes and crate-diggers everywhere, all hail Record Store Day!

—Larry Jaffee, July 2021, NYC

CAST OF CHARACTERS
(in alphabetical order)

Kim Bayley: Currently chief executive of the London-based Entertainment Retailers Association, Kim Bayley first joined ERA in 2002 and in two years rose to the organization's top position. She oversaw the United Kingdom's participation in Record Store Day in 2009.

Tom "Grover" Biery: The distribution group Warner/Elektra/Asylum's former "vinyl guy," Grover spearheaded the major label's backing for Record Store Day at the very beginning. He now operates the all-analog reissue label Slow Down Sounds.

Gerhard Blum: As Sony Music International's senior vice president of global distribution and supply chain, "Gerd" Blum oversees the manufacturing and distribution side of the business. During his twenty-eight years with the major, he's been astounded by vinyl's comeback.

Jeff Bowers: A former consultant to Warner Music Group. Along with Michael Kurtz, a driving force to make Record Store Day happen in its early days. He now is an artist manager, who's signed TikTok artists to major label deals.

Chris Brown: An executive at the Maine-based Bull Moose record store chain.

Michael Bunnell: Longtime leader of the Coalition of Independent Music Stores (CIMS), one of three coalitions of independent record stores, who helped form the basis for Record Store Day. Michael Bunnell also operates The Record Exchange, a store in Boise, Idaho.

Bryan Burkert: Owner of the Baltimore and Syracuse record stores The Sound Garden. The Baltimore location hosted Noise in the Basement, where Record Store Day was greenlit on September 23, 2007. The rest is history.

Carrie Colliton: One of only two people for whom the subject of this book is a full-time project. A cofounder of Record Store Day and marketing director for the coalition The Dept of Record Stores.

Amy Dorfman: A cofounder of Record Store Day, Amy Dorfman is a long-time marketing executive of Newbury Comics.

Steve Duncan: At both Rasputin Records and Zia Records, Duncan was instrumental in several key components of early Record Store Day, including the first in-store appearance from Metallica and the record store in the desert at Coachella.

Billy Fields: Currently Warner Music Group's vice president of sales and account management and is the vinyl point person for the company. His @billysezvinyl Twitter account often tells the story of vinyl sales by the numbers.

Lisa Foster: Co-owns Guestroom Records with locations in Oklahoma and Kentucky.

Rand Foster: Owner of Fingerprints, in Long Beach, California, the site of numerous in-store appearances including a set from The Foo Fighters. Foster also served as executive producer of RSD's first own vinyl release in 2017, *Like A Drunk In A Midnight Choir: A Tribute to Leonard Cohen,* and is a founding member of CIMS.

David Godevais: In 2002 David Godevais founded CALIF, a distribution network for independent French music labels.

In April 2011, he created "Disquaire Day," the French version of Record Store Day.

Matt Harmon: Two years after graduating college, Matt Harmon joined the Beggars Group, working his way up to President of its US operations of the major independent label umbrella, including its XL, 4AD, Rough Trade, and Young Turks.

Spencer Hickman: Formerly with Rough Trade record stores in the UK and New York, Spencer Hickman ran Record Store Day in the UK in 2009 to 2012. He is now creative director of Death Waltz Recording Company/Mondo Records and owns the record store Transmission.

Stephanie Huff: Former general manager of The Exclusive Company, a Wisconsin-based record chain founded in 1956. Attended the meeting that brought about Record Store Day.

Jan Koepke: Heading a team of six music enthusiasts, Jan Koepke coordinates Record Store Day in Germany, Austria, and Switzerland. He's worked in the music business since the 1990s.

John Kunz: A cofounder of CIMS, John Kunz owns the iconic Waterloo Records in Austin, where since 2008, he coordinates advertising and events for Record Store Day with all of Austin's many record stores.

Michael Kurtz: If the subject of this book was a television program, Record Store Day cofounder Michael Kurtz would be characterized as the "show runner." As the driving force behind RSD, Kurtz is known for his affable personality who relentlessly moves mountains within a record industry that isn't easily swayed. He also heads the Department of Record Stores (DORS), one of three retail coalitions that back RSD.

Eric Levin: Owner of Criminal Records in Atlanta, RSD cofounder Eric Levin also operates the Alliance of Independent MediaStores (AIMS) one of three retail coalitions that back RSD.

Josh Madell: Co-owner of the beloved indie record store Other Music, which was located across the street from a massive Tower Records location in Manhattan's Greenwich Village. He now works at Secretly Distribution.

Larry Mansdorf: A long-time buyer for Newbury Comics, RSD cofounder Larry Mansdorf represented the chain at the pivotal meeting that hatched Record Store Day.

Martin Mills: As founder of one of the world's largest independent label groups, Martin Mills first entered the record business by opening a shop. He then launched a label, Beggars Banquet, which led to 4AD, XL and other imprints, whose artists quickly embraced the Record Store Day concept.

Megan Page: Organizer of Record Store Day UK, Megan has brought the status of physical music formats back into British pop culture with initiatives including National Album Day

Marlien Parlievliet: The child of a Dutch record store family, Parlievliet spearheaded the effort to enlist one hundred indie record stores in The Netherlands into Record Store Day. She now owns a distribution company in Europe.

Andrea Paschal: General manager of the Coalition of Independent Music Stores (CIMS)—one of three retail coalitions that back Record Store Day. Paschal also oversees ThinkIndie distribution and manages RSD Summer Camp with Carrie Cotillon.

Dilyn Radakovitz: The former owner of the Dimple record store chain in Northern California, with her husband, Dilyn Radakovitz, was present at the September Noise in the Basement meeting in Baltimore, where RSD was greenlighted by fellow indie retailers. Dimple closed in 2019, but her son opened a store.

Donna Ross: A record industry veteran, Donna Ross currently is VP of sales for the Concord Music Group, and previously held management positions at Capitol/EMI, Caroline, 5.1 Entertainment, and the music marketing firm Ingrooves.

Portia Sabin: Currently president of the trade association/convention MusicBiz, Portia Sabin started her career as a punk rock drummer in NYC band The Hissyfits, then moved into artist management, and then ran the venerable independent record label Kill Rock Stars.

Jon Strickland: A champion of vinyl at two influential indie labels, Epitaph and Sub Pop, Jon Strickland witnessed firsthand how the rest of the record industry needed to catch up on giving the people what they wanted.

Don VanCleave: Besides being the founder of CIMS and the distribution firm Junketboy (later to be known as ThinkIndie), Don VanCleave went into artist management after twenty years of helping independent music retailers.

RSD Ambassadors

2009: Jesse "Boots Electric" Hughes (Eagles of Death Metal)
2010: Joshua Homme (Queens of the Stone Age, Kyuss, Eagles of Death Metal, Them Crooked Vultures)
2011: Ozzy Osbourne
2012: Iggy Pop
2013: Jack White
2014: Chuck D
2015: Dave Grohl
2016: Metallica
2017: St. Vincent
2018: Run The Jewels
2019: Pearl Jam
2020: Brandi Carlile
2021: Fred Armisen

LARRY JAFFEE is the cofounder of Making Vinyl, and is a New York–based journalist (larryjaffee. com), whose writing has appeared in *The New York Times, Rolling Stone, Billboard*, among numerous other publications. When not listening to music on vinyl, Jaffee teaches writing and journalism at local colleges.